Roll Strong(er)

Eric Falstrault

DEDICATION

To all those people who have supported me throughout my life, my beautiful kids Emily and Matthew, my parents and my mentors Charles Poliquin and Stephen Guy. I also want to thank those who have tried to slow me down, because they have made me who I am today.

TABLE OF CONTENTS

Roll Strong(er)

ACKNOWLEDGMENTS

To my kids. You give me the strength to wake up every day, looking forward to what's next, how you need my help and how I will have your backs for years to come, you are my life and my motivation and you keep me alive!

My late friend and mentor, Charles Poliquin, I owe it all to you. Up until you passed away you helped me. In your last conference, unknowingly, you made me stand up in front of everyone, just to tell them that I was the go to guy for anything mma, bjj and fighting sports. Never had the chance to thank you, but this book has a lot of your teachings in it. Forever grateful. See you in the next life.

This might be weird, but I have to thank some of my toughest and most hated teachers because they are the reason and the result of who I am today. My haters and those who made my life difficult, not believing in me or just trying to put me down, because I wouldn't be where or who I am today. Went through hell while writing this book, and fortunately, writing on a subject that is my passion probably saved my life more than once.

To my close friends. Anthony, James, Rita, Andrew T and Andrew P. You were always there when I needed it the most, drilling and rolling when I didn't have the strength to say a word. You gave me strength when I was at my weakest. You provided me with moral and emotional support in my life.

I am also grateful for my other family from Team Gracie Barra West Island and Professor Glen Mackenzie who always provides the best rolls and the best team one could ask for. My other family members and friends who have supported me along the way.

A very special gratitude goes out to all my BODHIFIT clients/friends. There is not a single day that I don't want to go to work and get to help you guys on your quests for better health.

Thanks for all your support!

Roll
Strong(er)

CHAPTER 1

WHEN IT ALL STARTED

There are so many BJJ success stories out there that can make you wonder if all of these are just a marketing scam. The fact of the matter is that I started reading them only once I was halfway through my white belt. I was getting crazy results regarding health, body and mind wise and as I started reading it, I came across to learn more of them.

You see, I am a trainer myself. I own a private facility, where I train athletes of all levels. My specialty is martial arts/fight sports, hockey, baseball, and soccer. I love training athletes because of their dedication and passion.

I am accustomed to what sport and physical activity can offer to others, but little did I know that I was going to be on the other side of the fence, where I needed to be.

Rewind to a great family vacation in Mexico in 2016. All went well until we got back. I started to feel bloated all the time and my sleep was the biggest problem, I just couldn't sleep anymore. When I say nothing, it was maximum an hour a night, and that's when I could sleep because some nights were just sleepless. It kept going, even though I tried almost everything to make it better. Holidays just made it worst, but I didn't give a shit and just kept eating and sleeping or trying to chill when I could. I just basically felt like shit and looked like shit, and I just didn't care. I never was one to be out of shape (round is a shape...). I guess that's what I lead myself to think. Although I believe that every personal trainer and coach out there should be in top shape, we coaches are not immune to bad health, circumstances and temptation.

I knew the longer I would wait, the worse it was going to be to get it back. I say it often to clients and I know all the tricks and tips to get back faster, but my mind didn't give a damn. In fact, my thoughts and thinking process were at the worst stage and I didn't like it. Something was wrong.

Holidays came to an end, and the pounds kept piling on, I decided it was enough. All the symptoms of intestinal dysbiosis were there. After a few weeks on probiotics and oregano oil caps, my digestion improved dramatically. The little nutrition clean up also made a great impact, but still not what I was expecting. I felt better, slept relatively better, but not as it should be.

Last time I did a transformation was the previous year. Did relatively well, but my bodyfat got stuck at around 17%, and for a trainers standard, it sucks. Life got in the way and I just cruised through summer by getting leaner but probably not where I should have been. This time, I did lose fat but only a bit.

In February 2017, I felt different (not in a good way) mentally and physically speaking. After almost 25 years of lifting weights, it has become a job. I call bullshit those who say that they enjoy working out as much as when they started. I would give you the same bull but I won't. Let's be honest, after a long while, you do it just because you know that if you let it go, you face dire punishment the moment you go back. You can't let go for too long because you pay the price. Even though sometimes life gets in the way, or there are days you don't feel like it and just want to lay down and do nothing, you know without a doubt that as soon as you are done with your lifting session, you'll be more than rewarded with a great feeling of accomplishment and wellness. The trouble is to get to the end of the session.

I was missing something.

I love helping people, it is a true passion. I started making programs for all kinds of people when I was 16 years old. I was the familiar face in the gym since I was there 7 days a week, at least 3 hours every single night. The passion for helping people get better and becomes a better version of them which never left me. However, keeping ourselves motivated after spending hours in the gym makes it challenging.

I knew I had to do something besides weightlifting. I needed some sort of a challenge or something to get my head out, a change.

Martial arts always was a great escape for me. Problem was that having a busy business left very little time for "me time". One mistake most trainers do is not taking enough time for themselves and not taking care of their own health. (Raising my hand shamelessly).

"If you can't go to the mountain, bring the mountain to you..."

I asked one of my BJJ athletes, Emmanuelle Ethier if she knew someone that could come and give private lessons to me and my staff at the gym. A week later, I met Andrew Prata, who is teaching at a Gracie Barra and was able to come at the exact time that I wanted, my downtime around 3 pm. We started with 2 classes a week to now a full 6 days a week.

I still do my weight lifting workouts around 3-4 days a week but since I fight almost everyday, I do weights in the morning and BJJ in the late afternoon.

I also tried my hand at the competition. I tagged along with 4 of my athletes to see and feel the whole process and how to prepare for it. I wanted to come a better trainer for them by completely immersing myself into it. In the field, they say that a coach cannot be a good athlete and vice versa. Let's see how we can reverse that myth.

What this book is all about

This book will be a helping guide for you, it will guide you all the way in your game. To gain the physical abilities that it requires and mostly, to help you enjoy rolling with all the little injuries that might come your way, if not already well established. This sport isn't much safer than others. You obviously have more chance of getting hurt than if you stay home on the couch.

Before you start being comfortable on the offensive, you'll have to play defensive, for a long while, against your opponent, his strength, his techniques (or lack of) and the goal, is to train for as long as you can, for the love of this amazing sport.

This book will help the beginner and even the advanced practitioner. It will improve your game, and even, prolong your rolling career for as long as possible.

The thing is that you probably heard that strength is your enemy in JITS, that having too much muscle mass can even impair your game and technique, make you less flexible when you need it the most. Those are very ignorant statements when it comes to sport, even more, when it comes to self-defense as if there will only be challenges you can overtake. As you will learn in this book, there are two types of muscle hypertrophy, sarcoplasmic and myofibrillar. One has more of a strength/hypertrophy ratio which is very useful and more functional for sports than the other. All you need to know for now is that for this sport, you need a mix of relative strength, functional hypertrophy and at times, muscular endurance. You might gain muscles, but don't be fooled into thinking that as soon as you spend some time lifting weights that you'll gain 10 lbs of lean muscles, it really, really doesn't work that way. This myth is outdated and shared by those afraid of hard work, plain and simple.

In BJJ, lifting should be considered a plus, as injury prevention and to help gain speed, stamina and yes, strength. You'll need it when you will be in the absolute division of your next competition. You'll need it when facing much bigger opponents. You'll need it when you'll be facing opponents that have more experience than you, just to survive and hold off chokes and arm bars. You'll need it more often just to survive. But most of all, if you are a BJJ junkie, an addict, you'll probably want to roll for as long as life can let you. You probably want that black belt as much as I do. To achieve that, you'll need a lot of guts and glory, with the body that follows. You need to be strong, healthy and wise. A healthy body, a strong mind. The longer you can maintain a good set of muscles, the better and longer you'll be in this game. But in general, as we grow older, we lose muscles and our metabolism slows down. We don't want to slow down, we want to get better or at least, slow down the aging process. Do it for JITS and your health's sake.

What I hope that you'll gain from reading this book is the necessary knowledge, not only about how to better your Jiu-jitsu game, but how to prevent injuries, get stronger, wiser, faster and healthier.

Why are my advices and tips as good as anybody else?

I have been training for more than 3 decades and helping people attain their goals in many sports for more than 20 years. To this day, I still study and keep on learning all I can for the love of sports and how to make people stronger, faster and healthier.

I have gained my strength and conditioning stripes with experience. In fact, I'm a coral belt in strength training if you compare it to BJJ. Not because I trained myself for a while, far from it. I spent thousands of hours training people, one on one, from all walks of life. I have also spent thousands of hours learning from the best there in strength and conditioning. I have trained Olympians, one of which is Martin Brodeur from the New Jersey Devils. I also have trained David Loiseau, one of the most talented and hard-working individuals to enter the UFC. I also have trained young athletes and old executives starting a new lifestyle. All of which had one goal in common, getting better at what they do, be more efficient and gain a healthier body along the way.

My job is to take a sport, and de-assemble it in pieces, determine what are the needs, specificities, uniqueness for each element of the sport and do the same with the person, the athlete in front of me. Put the puzzle pieces together to get a better athlete for his sport. I have to bring the best out of athletes. It might be for hockey, baseball, figure skating, combat sports or any other sports out there. I have to plan ahead of time for a given date and be of absolute certainty that they will be able to perform with the best of their abilities.

I have seen many of my athletes compete, train, hard, too hard or not enough. I have seen some great rolling and some not so great sessions where everything went wrong, mentally and physically. Understanding when to train and when you should just chill and drill is best. Forget about those who tell you that you abso'freakin'lutely roll every single day, twice a day, if you want to get better. Like any strength training program, diet, lifestyle, etc, it's case by case, no one is the same.

Is there any magical formula? No. Is there a way to find out if what you are doing is giving you better results? Hell yes! Am I going to give you the answer? No one can. The only person who can deal with it and figure it out is you. Even if you find it, the perfect program, it doesn't even mean that it will produce the same results twice.

Even if you find the numbers, the perfect program, and frequency, they might work for a while, but will it forever? It never does. It is called adaptation. One of the basic principles of training. Your body adapts to given stress by getting stronger. But life on the other end always plays tricks on us, or for a lack of better wording, it can easily get in the way. Meet a new someone in your life, get a new job, kids, injuries, new goals. All these can have a major impact and your body rarely does follow what life throws at it, it has to adapt first. This is where trainers usually come in.

If you have been rolling for a little while, you probably had those days where you felt like every roll was as if you were like in the movie Matrix? Like the scene where Neo was getting shot at and saw every single bullet coming and were able to let them pass by him in slow motion. Well these types of rolling sessions are memorable. They are usually the result of a rested mind and body. The perfect alignment of the physiological and psychological gods of rolling. I've found it is the same in Jits than it is in strength and conditioning. When the perfect conditions are met, get ready for great results.

Embrace those sessions. I would greatly suggest you write down a few notes. How you felt, what went on and anything you can remember about the previous days. Look at what you ate, how you slept and some of the techniques you drilled. Some of it could be part of greater and better rolling and/or training sessions.

Unfortunately, there will also be some sessions where you felt like a T-rex trying to land a Kimura or that you could not pass any one's guard even if it was a question of life or death. When you mess up parts of the plan, shit hits the fan. You can eat well, train properly but mess up a couple of nights of sleep, by your fault or just plain lack of sleep, and you become the T-rex or "I shall pass your guard". Same as the great classes, figure out what went wrong. Learn everything you can from them. The lessons that hurt (especially the ego) are the ones you learn the most from.

Embrace those sessions.

Those sessions teach you a lot and are probably the ones you can gather the most information to give to your new coach. This kind of information is invaluable. You now have a strength and conditioning coach.

Here is what you will gain from this book;

A better understanding of your own body and how it works
Improved stamina through well-designed conditioning programs
Healthier joints
Stronger and more focused rolls.
On point nutrition
Improved sleep
Insane body composition

Here's to your long-lived BJJ career!!!

CHAPTER 2

YOUR NEEDS

Most athletes come to see me when they are at the end of their rope. One soccer player came in with 5 knee ops to repair ACL tears and was on his way to a sixth and last one before hanging up his shoes. Don't be like that guy.

However, I had another one that came in after his knee exploded (literally) when his knee collided with another player during a game. After the operation, it took me 6 months to bring him back on his feet and running again. Be like this guy.

Unfortunately, some of them come to see me (or someone trustworthy) too late.

Failing to see and take care of some nagging little pains will always result in bigger and sometimes, irreversible problems. I would suggest something even better though, why would you wait until something happens.

A chain is only as strong as its weakest link.

In classes, I've seen some guys leaving limping, shoulder pains, neck issues, weak grips, low back discomfort, you name it... The fact of the matter is this, it is not how or where you will get hurt, it is when. You can be careful all you want, but you aren't rolling alone. Sometimes, it's neither of you guys fault, it could be just a bad move. Can you prevent that, absolutely not.

What if I tell you that all these joint issues can be lessened, even prevented? What if you can be able to prolong your rolling days for as long as you can? Now I'm just talking about preventing injuries.

The first thing Eddie Bravo said after rolling with Marcelo Garcia is that he, himself, has to get stronger. Garcia is a bull, that's his style, Eddie couldn't stop him. That's when he realized that strength is essential, especially that, as he said, he is not getting any younger so he has to get stronger to be able to roll with this style or stronger opponents.

The major problem I see nowadays is that people associate strength with big muscles. I have seen big weak guys and small strong as f**k guys. Strength also neither means lack of flexibility nor big muscles.

So where do we go from here? What do you need the most? Let's get it on!

First things first, let's evaluate your needs.

-Are you sore after working out?
-Do you have joint pains?
-Do you have difficulty sleeping after hard sessions?
-Do you feel out of shape when you try to kick it up a notch?
-Do you feel like you should have more flexibility?
-Do you feel like you should get stronger?
-Do you eat, on average 2-3 meals a day?

Well, if your answer is yes to one or more of these questions, you guessed it, you need to update your plan. Nutrition, habits, training, and the whole shebang.

Although everyone I meet goes through a thorough evaluation, reading a book can't obviously give you all the answers and an individualized approach. However, you can at least start with the basics and work your way up. For those who are advanced, going back to the basics is always a great idea and those who never set foot in a gym before will be off to a great start. I'll focus on what I see the most as issues in my practice and what I know can give you the unfair advantage as a Brazilian JiuJitsu practitioner.

Before trying to identify your needs, let's have a look at what the sport requires.

There are three main qualities that can influence what you need to plan in your training for a given sport. Force, speed and endurance.

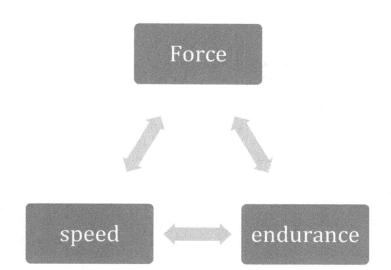

Unless you are a superhero, you can't have all the skills. There is an inverse relationship for all three. You can't have force or strength indefinitely because endurance and strength both are on opposite spectrums. Strength and power can last between 1 and at most, 20 seconds before it starts to jump into strength endurance. Even though you can lose pure strength after 20 seconds, the inverse relationship between strength and endurance starts to kick in. So you start losing strength slowly.

This is trainable though, but the maximum torque you have when you start to roll can't be kept indefinitely. This is why you see the white belts gassing out after a few minutes of their first few rolls. They use their strength like crazy since technique has not settled in and experience needs to be acquired. A normal and required process everyone needs to experience at first to really grasp why technique is essential.

N.B. Once you get into your first competition, technique goes out the window again and stress takes over, and again, you will gas out fairly fast for the same crazy reason, but another factor is involved, adrenaline. Your strength will be even more efficient, maybe too much, but it will cost you again on your endurance. Gaining experience is the goal and fortunately, a never-ending process.

Do you need to become bigger, leaner or stronger? The training approach would be much different for all three, but you'll end up training harder and discover all aspects of what the sport needs.

Depending on your actual body weight, I wouldn't worry about gaining a lot of muscle mass because unless you are a freak of nature (no you are not), you'll probably gain lean muscle mass very slowly. The fact of the matter is that as you train more, your caloric expenditure will probably take a beating so you'll probably end up in a deficit most days. So no worries the focus is on strength training, but we will also have a section for those wanting to gain lean muscle mass for competition or for pure pleasure.

Let's just say that you never touched a barbell or free weight before and it's your first time stepping into a gym. You might be the lucky one who never had issues. One thing is on your side, you won't be tempted to use too much strength and will focus more on technique, hopefully. However, keep in mind that you might have an increased risk of getting injured since your joints, ligaments, and tendons are lacking the strength needed to protect the joints, which is the main goal of this book.

The fact of the matter is this, I have never met any individual that never had any joint issue and if not, there was always some kind of strength discrepancy going on. It could be from top to bottom or from left to right, which is basically how problems start.

Posture is the bigger issue here. Phones, Ipads, computers or just work-related tasks make us more susceptible to injuries or some type of overuses. Take someone who works in a factory, for example, repetitive movements are part of everyday tasks. If you sit in front of a computer 8 hours a day, your posture is bound to pay the price, no matter how great your posture is while working.

Put that aside, as you become active, it often gets worse since those discrepancies become more apparent. That is the number one reason why you are always more comfortable drilling a technique on one side more than the other. This is why you can't seem to shake off that little nagging shoulder injury that you had for weeks.

While identifying your needs may look simple, gaining speed and strength or losing fat, identifying your weakest links can only help you prevent more serious injuries. If there is only one thing I wish you can gain from this book the knowledge of strength and conditioning for BJJ should be mainly aimed at preventing injuries which is the number one reason why most people quit in the first place.

Where most strength and conditioning specialized books fail miserably at is give you a good foundation. There is what we call the big 4: the bench press, the deadlift, the pull/chin-ups and the squats. I started training with these four lifts, which I can solely thank for my strength, 30 years later. However, as I gained strength and practiced many martial arts and many other sports such as track and field, injuries and sports individual needs will bring some joint issues along the way. As with many athletes, I trained and became stronger with bilateral lifts such as the big four but unilateral discrepancies slowed me down.

You are as strong as your weakest link. You have the major muscle groups and those who help to support them, which we often refer as stabilizer muscles. You have the pecs, shoulders, and deltoids that fire up strong for pushing while the lats, external rotators and neck extensors assist and stabilize the joint for proper range of motion.

As we try to push harder with bilateral lifts, the weakest link in the chain will hold us back, and as you push through it, that link will break. It doesn't stop there, unfortunately, especially when you don't take care of it.

immediately. These little injuries have the power to create a whole chain of problems with all the surrounding muscle groups and nerves, and if not taken care of, they can last a lifetime. It would be irresponsible for me not to try and find a way of giving tips and exercises to address these issues to help you drill and roll injury-free and for those who are already injury-prone or injured, I hope this book can help you find and fix those nagging aches and pains.

There are many ways to identify weaknesses. Simple movement screenings and muscle testing can be done, which is what we call « functional screening ». We use these simple tests to assess faulty movement patterns and discover the underlying cause. I will try to give you the simplest and most useful tools to help you identify these strength discrepancies and give you a good base to move forward.

The basics

For those who are new to lifting weights or never been active before undertaking BJJ, I suggest you to start by testing out your abilities with these basic lifts. I will also give you some guidelines as to where you are currently sitting with your conditioning and how to move-on from there. You will even find at the end of this section a table where you can keep and track your scores. I suggest you redo them a few months from now to compare and see what could be improved.

Some of these tests might be very basic and others might require a minimum of equipment, that you can easily find in a gym.

Let's get down to it…

Muscular tests

Push up test
Equipment needed: Stopwatch

For him or her, the rules are the same. The aim of this test is to perform as many push-ups as you can, with strict form in one minute. The starting position is with your arms straight, elbows locked, body straight, hands placed shoulder-width apart with fingers pointing forward and both feet on the floor (toes). For girls, they have the option of doing them on their knees due to upper body strength discrepancy. From the starting position, lower yourself until your chest TOUCHES the floor and your elbows should fall naturally back towards your feet. If your chest does NOT touch the floor, it does not count.

1.3 Push up scores for men

Age	17-19	20-29	30-39	40-49	50-59
excellent	56+	47+	41+	34+	31+
average	19-34	17-29	13-24	11-20	9-17

1.4 push up scores for woman

Age	17-19	20-29	30-39	40-49	50-59
excellent	35+	36+	31+	25+	23+
average	11-20	12-22	10-21	8-17	7-14

Source: www.topendsports.com

However, the push-up test is more of a functional/endurance type of test. For those who have access to a gym, here is how to test your maximum weight for 1 repetition on the benchpress. Maximum strength is what we are looking for. If you are able to push your way out of trouble, you only do it once, so building up strength is key. The 1 rep max test should be seen as a marker. If you can benchpress 200lbs and 3 months later you increased it by 40lbs, progress is there, and overall strength will follow. So keeping this score as an overall mark will help you track progress.

However, if you have less than 1 year of serious strength training under your belt (weight lifting belt that is), you shouldn't even try to test your 1 RM since your nervous system, biomechanics and coordination are not well prepared and can only alter the results, and you obviously have a higher risk of injury by performing your maximum weight.

1 repetition maximum close grip bench press strength test

This test was shown to me by my mentor and friend Charles Poliquin, world-renown strength coach of many Olympian and trainer of Helen Maroulis who at the 2016 Summer Olympics in Rio de Janeiro, Brazil she became the first-ever American to win a gold medal in women's freestyle wrestling at the Olympic Gamesi.

For the needs of the sports we will use a biacromial width (shoulder width) on a flat benchpress. As we learn very quickly in BJJ, elbows in, so testing the benchpress with the traditional elbows out benchpress for chest would be useless. The biacromial grip targets more the front deltoids and triceps and also the pectorals, but to a lesser percentage.

You absofreakinlutely need a spotter for this test. I repeat you need a spotter for this test.

You want to build up slowly to your max weight. So this is how it would look on paper. Use the following reps for each set.

1.5 1 rep max score sheet

1	2	3	4	5	6	7	8	9	10
4 reps	3 reps	2 reps	1 rep	1rep	1 rep	1 rep	1rep	1rep	1rep
30%	50%	65%	70%	75%	80%	85%	90%	95%	100%

It should take you about 10 sets to reach your max. Only your last set should be your absolute max. One critical detail should be the tempo or the speed of the repetition. Always keep a tempo 4010, 4 seconds to lower the bar, let the bar touch the chest and immediately lift it up as fast as you can without bouncing the bar on your chest. If the bar does not touch your chest, it doesn't count. If the spotter lifts the bar, you failed. You absolutely have to lift the bar by yourself. If it's your true max rep, you won't be able to explode the bar up, it might even take you more than a few seconds, but as long as you can rack it up, you are good. The spotter (a good one) should only grab the bar if it is going back down or you call it quits. Again, if you are injured, for obvious reasons, don't do this test.

Between set 1 to 3, you can rest only 1 minute but as soon as you start doing only 1 rep on set 4, you rest 3 minutes between each subsequent sets until you reach your max weight for 1 repetition. You could reach your max on set #8 which is fine but if you reached your true max on the fourth set, you overshot your weight. When it says 70%, it means that you can easily do 6 reps but you only do one. This is what we call ramping up. Slowly getting the weight up to max, see it as a big warmup. Lessens the chances of injuries.

Write it down and retest in 6 months to measure progress.

Abdominal strength

2 minute sit-up test (APFT)

The core muscles is the big Kahuna in jits. When You will be drilling those arm bar, triangle, omoplata, or ashi garami's, your abs will be screaming in pain. Don't worry, technique will sink in and abs strength and endurance will get much better. But if you want to see if you have some work to do for the core, this is one good test that will give you some indications. Nothing better than the Army physical fitness test as proving ground.

Lay on your back with your knees bent so that your ankles are about 12 inches from your buttocks or a 90° angle at the knees. You will have to anchor your feet under something or have someone hold your feet down to perform this test and your fingers have to be interlocked behind your head. The goal is to complete as many sit-ups in two minutes. Start the sit-ups by raising the upper body, beyond vertical (base of your neck is above the base of your spine) and then lower the body until the shoulder blades and the back of your hands touch the ground. Posing to rest is only permitted in the upright position.

Test score 2min sit-ups test

60+	elite
40-59	good
20-39	average
-20	poor

Source: www.topendsports.com

Ankle and knee flexibility

Before we start talking and testing lower body strength, one of the most common injuries in grappling sports is lower back/knee related. Both are usually related since a strength discrepancy between both hamstring or/and lower can render the knee unstable due to unwanted load during training and rolling.

When it comes to strength training, squats, deadlifts and Olympic lifts are the kings of movements. Big movements pay big dividends. However, having issues with a knee or lower back, especially if you train over them is just like playing Russian roulette. I always evaluate the health of the knees before anything happens and I start making a program.

Being able to fully bend the knee is somewhat of a lost art because of faulty information that is spread around by shitty trainers who are scared of their own ability to coach effectively. This often leads to injuries. They rather believe age-old myths like the knee can't pass the toes while squatting down instead of learning how to properly squat and how to fix issues when someone can't.

Knee and ankle flexibility is a great concern for many. When you start to practice your stand-up game, that is where most people knees get a beating. When Hip throws and landings go wrong, they can put you out for a long while. The goal is to prevent and make your knees as stable and strong as possible. In order to do so, one must achieve structural balance, as in all muscles of the thighs and hip should be able to perform full range and strength in motion.

Simple rule, your hamstrings should be able to touch your calves at the bottom of a squat .

Now, most people can't achieve that on their first few sets. Faulty postural patterns, past injuries or just bad technique can be the culprits. I and most of my esteemed colleagues don't even include squats for the first few months of training. We first determine the major cause of concern and correct it.

For those who don't have the luxury of hiring a strength coach, there are ways to know if you have faulty biomechanics. Word of caution, if you had any injuries in one or both knees, I would highly suggest you get advice or an evaluation from a therapist or strength coach and not try to self evaluate yourself. This simple exercise can tell you a lot about what has to be done first. A simple split squat can tell you a lot.

The goal is to bend the front knee all the way until the back of the leg touches the calf.

If you feel a stretching in the hip of the back leg, it is normal. If you feel that it is limiting your range of motion and start bending forward to compensate, you found problem #1, tight hips flexors.

If you are unable to go all the way down or just feel uncomfortable with the knee or pain, stop right there and go right away with the rehab and prehab program in the training section, phase one white belt, same goes with problem #1. Ankle flexibility could also be a problem and can usually be fixed with ankle exercises which is also part of the rehab/prehab program.

Another pattern we often see is that the knee falls inwards, which is a weakness in the vastus medialis muscle, aka V.M.O., tear drop like muscle on the inside of the knee that contributes to correct tracking of the patella.

Obviously, this is not a strength test per say, but it is one of the most important test for grapplers and wrestlers since lower body strength and flexibility is a big part of your longevity in this sport. The goal of the rehab/prehab program included in this book helps recover structural balance and flexibility of the ankle, knee and hip joints. Even though you might pass this test with flying colors, but never lifted weights previously, I would still suggest that you start with the rehab/prehab program and start with a good base. I would suggest the same for the more advanced athletes since going back to the basics once a year is never a bad idea and can prevent further injuries.

Now, for those with knee injuries, a simpler and safer test can be done. Most of us have a staircase in our houses and that is all you need. You could also use a small step, stool or bench. Put one foot on the step, and step 5 times each leg. A great visual aid would be that you set a camera or your phone in front of you, to see how your body reacts as you go up. If your upper body wiggles from one side to the other and you seem to lose balance, your lower back could be a concern. The quadratus lomborum, deep core muscles attached to the low back and hip are not firing properly and making you unstable. If your knee buckles in again, VMO is the weak muscle. As with the split squats, you can have only one knee that buckles in which is fine. You have found a unilateral discrepancy.

For this test, if you are using a bench, the higher it is, more difficult it will be. For the step-up test, get one that is about mid-calf level. If the step is too high, you probably will bend forward. However, even if the bench is high and your knees don't buckle in and you don't bend forward, you pass this test.

Pull up strength test

Pulling strength is, in my opinion, the most important of all of them in grappling sports for obvious reasons. Arm drags, takedowns and throws, ground game, chokes and holds, pulling your opponent is what you'll do the most. Pull-ups are one of the 4 basic moves in strength and conditioning with deadlifts, squats, and presses. It also gives a great insight on grip strength, the most neglected muscles in strength and conditioning.

Grab a high bar with palms facing away (or pronated grip) shoulder-width apart. You must start with your arms completely straight hanging down from the bar. Raise yourself until the chin clears the top of the bar, then lower yourself again to a position with the arms fully extended. The pull-ups should be done in a smooth motion. No jerking motion, swinging, and kicking and bending the legs are forbidden. Do as many pull-ups as possible.

There are no norms established for pull-ups, but consider this, if you want to be a United states marine, you have to perform at least 3 strict pull-ups. A navy SEAL should do at least 8 but 15-20 is recommended which makes more sense in my humble opinion. You've got guys like Barstarzz cranking out 20-30-50 reps easily and smiling.

By chance, the President's Council on Fitness, Sports, and Nutrition has some standards:

Children – 6-12 years of age should perform between 1-2 pull-ups (i.e. 50th percentile).

Teens – boys 13-18 years of age should perform between 3-8 pull-ups (i.e. 50th percentile, girls 13-18 years of age should perform 1 pull-up or a 5-9 second flexed arm hang.

Adults – Hard to find data but average Men should perform a minimum of 8 pull-ups, with 13-17 reps considered fit and strong. Women should perform 1-3 pull-ups, with 5-9 reps for fit and strong.

Flexed arm hang test

This is more of a challenge than a test but still relevant to our sport. Even though the flexed arm challenge bears a resemblance to the pull-up test, when requires reps and the other an isometric hold. Grab an overhead bar with your palms facing away from the body grip (pronated grip) with a shoulder width grip on the high bar. Position the body with the arm flexed and the chin clearing the bar and the subject has to be helped to get into position to decrease extra exertion. The chest should be held close to bar with legs hanging straight. Start the timer as soon as the chin clears the bar and timing is stopped when student's chin touches or falls below the bar. A minimum of 15 seconds is required to pass the test. Marines are awarded 1 point for every 1 second up to 40 seconds, then 2 points per second, have fun with that.

Handgrip Strength Test

This one is a little harder to come by but well worth the search. Try to find a coach who owns a dynamometer. The purpose of this test is to measure the maximum isometric strength of the hand and forearm muscles. Handgrip strength is the key to every BJJ athlete. Also, as a general rule people with strong hands tend to be strong elsewhere, so this test is often used as a general test of strength.

Grip strength is also a strong cardiovascular disease predictor for people of various economic and socio-cultural environments. These results suggest that muscle strength is a risk factor for cardiovascular disease and can even predict the risk of death in people who develop cardiovascular disease or not. What should we learn from this? The actual grip has nothing to do with the research though. Those who had a better grip were the strong ones, meaning they were most active and kept their strength alive. The take-home point is to strength train, which makes a body good and strong overall. Everybody needs more grip strength.

Cardio vascular tests

Burpee test

There is nothing that comes to mind that sucks more than the burpees, but they actually work and for testing, they are the bomb. It test strength endurance, agility, balance, and coordination. All you have to do is do as much as you can in 30 seconds.

The starting position should be standing with arms by your side. Squat down, put your hands in front than thrust your legs back to a push-up position. Bring your legs back and then jump up with your arms reaching up then squat back down and so on.

There are two possible tests for this which you should start with the basic one. Do as much as you can for 30 seconds. A good result for a 30-second test is >16 burpees for men and >12 for women.

For the hardcore and willing freaks, especially those who like a challenge, do the 5 minutes one. For those trying their hands at the competition, go for this one since most rounds average 5 minutes. Adults need to get over 80 (women) or 85 (men) in five minutes.

500 M and 2k rowing test

I use these tests to completely exhaust all energy production pathways to mimic competition and full-on rolling sessions. Good for maintenance with those with little injuries that prevent them from rolling. Always pulling for 7-8 minutes and the fact that you are crouched up makes it harder to breathe, the same as when you are getting crushed under side control or mounted and out of breath. The concept 2 rower is the best tool since it records the scores and the data is well indicated.

For the test, just do cover the distance as fast as possible. The 500 meters is more for strength endurance and the 2K is for all-out war on aerobic endurance and guts.

If you look at the concept 2 rower online rankings, the average in 2017 for man is 1 minute 43 seconds for the 500 M and 7 minutes 45 seconds for the 2K. For women, 2 minutes 4 seconds for the 500 M and 8 minutes 57 seconds for the 2K. Considering that they all train on the rower, probably extensively before they even put up a score, trying to reach the average is a good mark for BJJ athletes.

The plank test

The plank endurance tests measure the control and endurance of the core and lower back muscles. All you need to do is hold an elevated position for as long as you can. On your elbows, forearms, and feet, you lift up your hips so that it forms a straight line from head to toe.

1.7 plank test

Rating	Time	
Excellent	+6 minutes	
Average	1-2 min	
Poor	15-30 sec.	

The record is over 30 minutes but it is useless in my opinion. Abs are made to be strong, and well trained to support a resistance greater than it can hold. My rule of thumb is this, if you feel your lower back is uncomfortable after a minute or so, consider working your core and lower back the proper way, the way you will learn in your new workouts in the rehab and prehab section.

Flexibility

Hamstring and lower back

The Sit and reach test is done with a ruler and stairs. If you have completed the previous tests, you will be well warmed up by the time you do this test. Barefoot against the base of stairs or a flat surface with legs straight and toes pointing upwards. Place a ruler on the step and slowly bend forward and try to reach as far as possible with the tip of the fingers. Have someone mark down your score and try it again 2 or 3 times, putting down your best score. This test is useful to determine the flexibility of your hamstring and also great to measure progress each time around.

1.8 sit and reach scores

	Men (inches)	Women (inches)
excellent	10.5+	11.5+
average	0 – 2.0+	0.5 – 4.0
poor	-7.5 - -3.5	-6.0 - -3.0

Source: www.topendsports.com

To focus on speed, strength and power/strength, you need to split your workouts and make sure you time them well with your rolling sessions. But first we have to talk about what will be about 80% of your success. Without having the proper plan, especially adding a few strength and conditioning sessions on top of your BJJ sessions, you will have to focus on your habits first.

CHAPTER 3

HABITS

We often have a lot of good habits, which we focus on, and in fact, they are the foundation of your day. You get up in the morning, take a shower while your cup of coffee gets ready. Have breakfast, gather up your meal preps for the whole day. If the day goes well, you'll have eaten all your food, trained with all the energy in the world and once it's time to go to bed, you'll fall asleep with no problems whatsoever.

That should be your perfect day. However, can you honestly tell me how many days in a month would be close to your perfect days? If you say more than 10, you are the lucky chosen.

Unfortunately, life often throws us some curve balls, which we have to deal with the best of our abilities. We all know how we can have some sort of control over our good habits but recognizing what we should do when shit hits the fan is also a part of our learning curve.

Some of these habits are so obvious that we don't think they have such a huge impact, negative or positive, on our health and fitness.

A quick tip before we keep going. When you measure or weigh yourself, always do it on the same day and time of the week. Don't be the person who jumps the scale every single morning. Body weight could fluctuate by 10 lbs in a matter of days, putting you off balance (pun intended) for the rest of the week. Try that before competition, a real treat.

Now that we know how and when to measure progress, let's take a look at what you are doing now.

I believe that when someone makes changes in its lifestyle, a sudden wave of changes never lasts. It has to be done gradually, by changing only 1-2 habits at first, see what happens and move to the next one. I believe in finding the " worst" terrible problem (yes, I wrote that) in your daily habits because it's not only food that could be a trigger. Habits are what makes you who you are. It has a lot to do with nutrition habits but also sleeping, working and training habits that can influence your health. I always go in order of importance and this is how I will introduce them. I am a time saver. If I can save time by killing two birds with one stone, why not. I hate to waste my time so everything I do has to have a purpose. I do the same with my clients. I have to produce results as fast as I can, always keeping their health in mind.

One habit that has the most influence on our energy is **meal frequency**.

Train more eat more, that's very understandable, but what is the ideal meal frequency for JiuJitsu athletes? It depends on the goals and especially on the digestive system of each individual. It will never be a one size fits all plan so trial and error is the key for a successful approach to your own personalized protocol.

With that being said, the more you train and roll, the more you'll need to eat, but the concern is, when? Training while you are full is bound for disaster and while probably slow you down and rolling while hungry can make you gas out or just leave you with no energy. So timing is everything. Most classes are at lunch and after dinner. In my opinion, the most important meal of the day is breakfast.

First, if you eat erratically, at no given time during the day or like "the executives", you eat when you have time, this is a problem. I fix my schedule around my eating schedule. The first thing I know is when I'll be able to eat and train, then I move my work schedule around. The last meal of the day is about setting your body into rest mode. I always include more carbs on my later meals, which helps lower cortisol. Keep in mind that goals always set up the nutrition path. Might not be suited for all. Individualization is always the key.

In the Journal of Physiology and behavior, they demonstrated that;

•Changes in meal timing influence obesity and the success of weight loss therapy.

•Unusual feeding time can induce a disruption of the circadian system.

•Digestive enzymes express in a circadian manner and are synchronized by food.

•Feeding is the source of energy for adipose tissue. The time of feeding is decisive.

•Clock genes are important in meal timing by changes in circadian control of hunger.

In a recent 12-week study they showed that subjects who ate more calories during breakfast lost more weight than those who ate more calories at dinner. Furthermore, they also discovered that organs have an active circadian clock-related to food intake, in this case, the stomach, intestine, liver, and pancreas.

It might be new to the Pubmed and medical community but it is very old news to the Chinese medicine advocates which goes beyond the scope of this book.

Depending on goals, such as fat loss and weight gaining, you may have to cut carbs, add fat and protein, etc as you'll read in the nutrition section.

Another very important habit I would focus on is the **quality of your sleep**. That's not a big secret. With no sleep, everything seems harder, less focused, tons of coffee, etc. Actually, Americans are sleeping less and less for multiple reasons. The American Thoracic Society International Conference, 2006, showed that women who slept 5 hours per night were 32% more likely to experience major weight gain (an increase of 33 pounds or more) and 15% more likely to become obese over the course of the 16-year study, compared to those who slept 7 hours a night[ii]. This one is very simple to explain. Less sleep means lower leptin levels which bring on the cravings roller coaster. Since you have more time to eat, you go towards bad choices like sweets and junk. Lack of sleep interferes with your ability to metabolize carbs efficiently, it is much easier for your body to store body fat, increase your insulin resistance, your blood pressure and your risk of having heart disease.

Sleep is also when your body enters the regeneration and grow mode. After a few days of disturbed sleep, do you really think you can perform at 100%? You have to do a full day's work and then follow it with a few rounds of sparring and rolling. Then you wonder why you can't seem to finish that arm bar correctly or grasp the "technique du jour".

Most people tell me they sleep well, but the quality is in the eye of the beholder. For some 6 hours of sleep is enough and others can't function under 9 hours of sleep. 6 or 9, I opt for uninterrupted sleep. If one can sleep 6 hours of sleep uninterrupted and feel great upon waking up, that's my definition of quality sleep. As I said if you need 9, fine! As long as it is 9 hours without waking up a few times in between, it means that your body is resting and regenerating.

Now, most of you probably can't remember when you had a few good nights of sleep in a row. One of the most common problems in jits is lack of sleep. I get this complaint, and what I read the most in BJJ forums and threads, is that most can't seem to get a good night's sleep after rolling hard at night which is absolutely normal in my opinion. The adrenaline rush keeps us awake and kicking. We recall the good, but especially where we sucked, when we messed up and what we should have done better. Thankfully, there are a few things that can help you get a better night's sleep.

Tips for quality sleep

1. Set the mood

Your mind is awake. Going on Youtube to search for butterfly sweeps escapes is not what I call setting up the mood to chill and get ready to hit the sack. Any type of blue light (computer, Ipads, and phone)[1] has the ability to disturb your sleep. Exposure to this type of light at night suppresses the secretion of melatonin, a hormone responsible to regulate the circadian rhythm. A slight change in your circadian rhythm can negatively impact blood sugar metabolism and throw off leptin levels, which as you read earlier, can have a serious impact on your health. In contrast expose yourself to blue or bright light during the day. This will keep you awake and focus ad help your circadian rhythm regulate itself and start shutting down at night when it should naturally.

So to set the mood and get your body to slowly get into sleeping mode, dim down all the lights, turn down all electronics 2 to 3 hours before bedtime. No TV watching in bed also. The bedroom is made for sleeping and … Never bring your laptop or watch a movie in bed. You are only mixing up the signals. Prior to bed, watch a boring movie and the best way yet is to read a book. Nothing exciting though. I know some of you are junkies, but studying techniques can be done early in the morning, anyway, you'll better retain the information than with your favorite cup of java and a nice steak and eggs breakfast to boost your dopamine levels.

2. Sleep aids.

---

[1] Says the guy who is writing this book after his kids are in bed and while his wife watches her favourite cooking shows. Thankfully, I do it with a special blue light screen saver.

I am not talking about Tylenol night or Nyquil. We talked about **Melatonin** in the last point and if you can't seem to fall asleep, this should be in your arsenal. The recommendation is usually 5 to 10 grams but I have had people go up to 25-30 grams but only for a few days until the cycle starts to go back to normal. A few days on that protocol and they felt that they didn't need it anymore. I find that the 5-10 grams work very well with almost everyone.

Another useful natural sleep aid I use is magnesium glycinate. Magnesium is a mineral involved in hundreds of processes in the human body and is important for brain function and heart health.

In addition, magnesium may help quiet the mind and body, making it easier to fall asleep[iii]. You often find it in combination with herbs such as valerian, passionflower, common herbs that help with insomnia. One of my favorite supplements I add to my pre-bed routine is **Optisom from ATP labs**, which has the perfect ration of magnesium, melatonin and all the natural herbs that eases the mind. Especially after those hard rolling sessions, you need to forget everything that went wrong and focus on the day ahead and the next drills and rolls.

Take it an hour or so before bed and get into your pre-bed ritual. You'll be catchin' some quality and more restful sleep.

3. Some answers to more restful sleep can be found in functional medicine. Your body speaks with symptoms. What is very common to you may be the answer to us. Let's say that you always have a hard time to fall asleep, which tells us that your cortisol, the stress hormone, is probably high at night when it should be low. The pre-bed routine and melatonin should be able to fix that.

You can't get out of bed in the morning without punching the snooze button a few times? Cortisol should be high in the morning, that's why you get up. But low morning cortisol is often the result of late-night snacking. Spending the night digesting impairs the rest and regeneration process that happens while you sleep. Late-night snacking is always the result of a lack of proper eating habits during the day.

One of the few habits that can be very rewarding and at times, can be very challenging is the proper use of REST DAYS. I don't know if the problem comes from peer pressure since most guys will tell you to roll and practice as much as you can, but listening to yourself instead of others can save a few years of your rolling life. We quickly become junkies as I can happily say that I can practice it every single day since I own a dojo inside my own gym and make my schedule and workouts around it. But I find that once in a while, if not because of injury, when I stop for a few days or a week at most, I feel that when I come back, everything is much clearer, the flow is incredible, even though I haven't even looked at videos or drill for the past week.

You can be at the dojo every single day and learn lots and to tell you the truth, we all fall for this. As we gain experience, we can feel when good and bad rolling days are on their way, this is the goldilocks zone. You know, those days where you can say that you felt great, rolled (almost) effortlessly and that all the moves came in quickly.

You can't say no to bad days and actually, it will be too late when you realize that it is one of them. Those days where you just feel like "this shit is not for me". When you roll and that lower belt finds all the freakin' spots where you just can't roll or submit. Well, those days, aren't the best, but they are those where you learn the most. Don't get angry, just let it sink in and learn from what happened. You'll be just one step closer.

This is where the importance of a training journal comes in handy. I'm sure you have seen people at the dojo with a little black book or note pad, writing done a few notes after class. Besides technique, this tool is amazing to figure out patterns. As you write down the dates of all the sessions you have done and a little rundown, I would suggest that you mark down on your calendar each time you went. Put down a red X on the days you felt great and a black X when you felt like crap.

Stretching

Stretching could be good but can also be overdone. As you have seen, in the evaluation of chapter 2, you might have issues with stretching. There are ways to stretch the muscles properly before and after sessions. However, most would love to become very flexible. Continuous stretching done lightly will get you there. It will take you a few weeks, more often years to see an amazing improvement. Like hypertrophy, flexible joints have a lot to do with genetics and also, nutrition. Yes, what you eat has also the greatest impact on how flexible and relaxed your muscles are. I would say that nutrition is one of the main issues when inflammation of the joints appear.

Wait a minute, muscles? Yes, you read that right. Injuries (past or present) and posture dictate tight and relaxed muscles. Big guys who only benchpress would have tight pectoral muscles and the upper back would appear weak or loose because of a lack of strength due to overpowering of the front plane, which in this case is the pectoral and front deltoid muscles.

What would be tight in BJJ fighters? Shoulders, upper back/neck muscles, low back, hamstrings, elbows, and wrists, to name a few. The problem is that once a little injury appears, it can trigger a whole chain of compensation from the surrounding muscles and joints.

Understand that stretching is not just loosening up what is tight. You have to understand the mechanics of injury. If a muscle is tight, something is initiating or triggering the pull. Think about an injury to the lower back. Twisting and torque in a bad position is often the culprit, however, the lack of flexibility made it worst and surrounding muscles had to pull to resist. If the hamstrings are either tight or weak, they won't be able to offer the least amount of resistance as protection, and that is when trouble arises.

Before stretching, especially if you never trained before, start by incorporating the first phase of the workouts, the rehab/prehab phase. Exercising in itself teaches the muscles how to relax. The workout is the contraction and stimulus followed by relaxation in the rest and regeneration for the next few hours and days. Also, as mentioned previously, nutrition plays a big part in the health of your muscles and joints. Combining these two new habits will have a positive impact on how flexible you can become, and you'll see a big difference in a matter of weeks. I often saw major differences with only a simple strength and conditioning program and simple changes in nutrition.

Eating at regular intervals

This simple habit is what should be a priority in your day. I set up my day around the time of when and where I should eat. Meal frequency might be more important than you think.

Train more eat more, that's very understandable information. But what is the ideal meal frequency for JiuJitsu athletes? It depends on the goals and especially on the digestive system of the individuals. It will never be a one size fits all plan so trial and error is the key for a successful approach to your own personalized protocol.

With that being said, the more you roll, the more you'll need to eat, but the concern is, when. You can't roll on a full stomach for sure. So timing is everything. Most classes are at lunch and after dinner. In my opinion, the most important meal of the day is breakfast. We'll get into greater detail in the nutrition section.

In the Journal of Physiology and behavior, they demonstrated that;

•Changes in meal timing influence obesity and the success of weight loss therapy.
•Unusual feeding time can induce a disruption of the circadian system, hence, sleep disturbance.
•Digestive enzymes express in a circadian manner and are synchronized by food.
•Feeding is the source of energy for adipose tissue. The time of feeding is decisive.
•Clock genes are important in meal timing by changes in circadian control of hunger.

Get organized, plan your day in advance. You should know when you can eat during your day. Plan your day around your feeding time. Sure, it sounds a bit crazy, but getting the results you want needs a little bit more effort than eating on the go. If your day and your first meal starting at 9 am, think of eating every 3 to 4 hours intervals from that time, which would be 12, 3 pm, and 7 pm.

Meal planning could be complicated in itself, especially for athletes. Give yourself an hour to digest before training or rolling. The heavier the meal, the harder it will be to digest, so the quantity might be something to plan ahead and it would be preferable to have it post-workout.

Stay away from modified foods.

This must be one of your top priorities. If you have tried the Paleolithic or Mediterranean Diet, you should have felt a difference fast enough. When we eat as close as possible to what our ancestors used to eat, it is almost impossible not to feel any difference.

There are countless reasons why you should avoid these foods. Perhaps because of the unpronounceable additives they contain or because they are often made from genetically modified foods (GMO) or because these products are the result of agriculture soaked in glyphosate.

Eliminating these fast, convenient foods from our diet requires new habits. It will take a little more time to cook our meals instead of just opening a small box and call it a meal. This small change of habit seems very time consuming, but the time spent preparing will be replaced by new health and performance.

Do not be surprised if I tell you that even our fruits and vegetables are in this category. Genetically modified foods are gradually entering our supermarkets, with a slightly different code.

Here are the basics of what you need to know:

If there are only four digits in the PLU code (Price lookup), this means that the product has been grown in a conventional or "traditional" way with the use of pesticides. The last four letters of the PLU code are simply the kind of vegetable or fruit. An example is that all bananas have the label with the code 4011.

If there are five digits in the PLU code, and the number starts with "8", it tells you that the item is a genetically modified fruit or vegetable. Thus, it is impossible to eat organic products that are grown from genetically modified seeds. A modified genetically modified banana (GE or GMO) would have the code 84011.

If there are five digits in the PLU code, and the number starts with "9", it tells you that the product has been grown organically and is not genetically modified. An organic banana would have the code 94011.

A lot of research is available on this subject and even the media are starting to talk about it and inform us about the potential dangers of this kind of genetic modification done on our food and products. The problem is that some of our media are funded by these same agriculture and pharmaceutical companies. There is a huge lobby, both on the nutritionists' side and in food media because greed will always take over health.

How can we suggest following the so-called food guide when the rate of obesity has been steadily rising for twenty years? It obviously is a problem but when we have huge corporations controlling the message, the main recommendations of the food guide pyramid, whom should we trust when it comes to knowing what to eat and how to be healthy?

By listening to what the government wants us to believe and take the easiest way?

It's not enough to just watch the late-night news, but most importantly, the commercials. You will only see ads of junk food and sweets, specially designed to make you succumb to temptation. The news is depressing most of the time so why not take down the cortisol (unconsciously) with potato chips or a good chocolate bar before going to bed? This way, you'll get upset the next morning, you'll be even more tired the next night and it's the beginning of a wheel that runs endlessly. Here's one more reason to turn off your TV in the evening or watch something else that's just as depressing from one night to the next.

When it comes to your health, your personal goals and needs, you can't pay attention to the general recommendations of the other people. The goal is to shop and eat healthy. Clean your fruits and vegetables before eating to eliminate pesticides. Buy local and organic products as often as possible. I agree it's more expensive, but the return on your investment will be quick.

Despite the claims of some nutritionists and dietitians, one of the first things that I eliminate with my clients - when I suspect digestive or intestinal problems - is GLUTEN. OH no!!! not another one who believes in this crap! Yes, I am one of those who believe that gluten is one of the major problems of our time. Each person is different, so its symptoms vary person to person. Some symptoms may appear a few weeks later, some immediately. From unexplainable skin irritation problems to food intolerance problems which are so-called healthy food choices. Who would want to believe that gluten can make you intolerant to other foods?

See the gut as a complex plumbing system. If some things like fat or meat remain in the tubing and block some parts, then gluten may be doing the same thing in some parts of your intestines. This will result in accumulations followed by blockage which will make this section of intestine somewhat less functional. Anything you eat later will be affected. These parts of the intestine will become sooner or later permeable, becoming antigens by penetrating the bloodstream, causing inflammations and food intolerances.

Even if you believe that gluten does not affect you at all, try to eliminate it for 30 days just to give it a try. If you see a clear difference in your ability to concentrate, digestion, a clear improvement in a recurring joint problem, or easy and unexplained weight loss, you have just found one of the major problems that kept you away from the results you wanted to get.

Same thing with milk. Thanks to growth hormone injections, cows increase their milk production yields by at least 15%, an average increase of one gallon, or 3.80 liters, per day. One consequence of the Posilac injection is the significant increase in mastitis, the udder inflammation that is quite common in high yielding herds. This inflammation makes sure that there is pus in the milk. According to a study conducted by the University of Vermont on a test group, the mastitis rate reached 40% in the group of cows treated with rBGH whereas it was only 10% among the control group, who was not receiving treatment.

These mastitis problems have another impact on the quality of the milk because to treat these inflammations, the farmers resort to injections of antibiotics whose residues are found in the milk. These same antibiotics are then found in the body of the consumer and participate in the development of pathogenic strains resistant to antibiotics.

One of the many lessons I learned from my colleague Mark Schauss is this: our body is like a gun and the toxins/chemicals are like the bullets we put in. With each exposure to one of these toxins, you insert a bullet into the barrel. One day, you get up and life pulls the trigger.

Last important habit but not the least…

Strength training

For jits, as I have said previously, popular beliefs seem to demonize strength training as unnecessary. The problem with this way of thinking is that yes, technique will often surpass strength, but strength can help you survive. Those with experienced rolling with less experienced ones have a much harder time with those who are strong than those who are weak right? Obviously. Why? Those who have a strong strength base can resist or get out of some compromising situations easier than those who don't for obvious reasons.

But more importantly, I would consider strength training and hypertrophy a plus for injury prevention.

Our body moves in multiple directions and performs movements, oftentimes, in unnatural ways while fighting, even just while drilling or discovering new techniques. Kimura's, Americana's and neck cranks are not what I can call natural in any form or imaginable way. By building strength, it increases our capacity and tolerance to withstand external load and forces while protecting our joints and other soft tissues. Resistance training also helps the activation of motor skills for function and movement.

If you need one more reason to start incorporating strength training into your weekly routine, slowing down the aging process should be one of them. Adults who don't lift can lose about 3 pounds of muscle every six years. Our metabolism slows down with age and we have to deal with the effect of growing old.

I like to see our tribe like a legion of gentle warriors. All I do is live to roll faster, better and learn as much as I can to better myself and to be a better Jujitsu Fighter. That's all I care about. As soon as I step on to the mats, all I did since I woke up in the morning, eating, thinking and working, are all added up into the perfect condition to roll in the afternoon. To be the best training partner while having a full tank of energy to roll like a mother roller. I have read one book that completely changed the way I think about health. We have control over ourselves all because of the habits we have.

The next lessons, taken from former warriors, are the basis of the code I follow and in my opinion, the quintessence of an accomplished existence of a healthy mind in a healthy body. If you have read my last book, The strength code, you can skip right to the next chapter which is nutrition.

The warriors are 24 hours a day, 7 days a week. They follow the path of samurai, Bushido2. Practicing the principles of sincerity, altruism, creativity, multiple forms of martial arts and ready to die at any time for the cause. This is what Hagakure's work highlighted. I came across similar readings to Hagakure3 at practically the same time. The difference is that instead of not valuing the life of a samurai, the author put a lot of emphasis on the health, physical and mental strength of the warrior. Kaibara Ekken, a fine samurai physicist with Buddhist influences, took a different approach. He understood that the physical, mental and spiritual aspects of great warriors are all interconnected, united and formed a whole. He looked at everything

---

[2] "Bushido", which literally means "the way of the samurai" is a modern rather than historical term. The way itself comes from the moral values of samurai, most often emphasizing a combination of frugality, loyalty, mastery of martial arts, and honor death. Born from neo-Confucianism in peacetime Tokugawa Japan and following Confucian texts, Bushido was also influenced by Shinto and Zen Buddhism, allowing the violent existence of samurai to be softened by wisdom, discernment, philosophy, and serenity.

[3] Practical and spiritual guide for a warrior, taken from a collection of comments by samurai Yamamoto Tsunetomo, former retainer at nabeshima mitsushige, the third ruler of what is now Saga Prefecture in Japan. Tsuramoto Tashiro compiled these comments from his conversations with Tsunetomo 1709-1716; however, it was published only many years later. Hagakure is often seen as a "way of dying" or living as if one were already dead, and a samurai must be ready to die at any time in order to be faithful to one's lord. His saying "the way of the warrior is dead" was of a summation of the will to sacrifice that codified bushido.

from nutrition to sexual practices, maintaining the shape and endurance of any age, excess, restraint, lifestyle and more.

The basic premise of Ekken is that we all have the ability to live to 100 years. What we do all these years will dictate if we will be able to live to celebrate our 100th birthday.

His ways of feeding life are still highly respected, even after 300 years. I strongly suggest you read his book Yojokun, Life Lessons from a Samurai. These lessons are not just for the ancient samurai. These habits will forge a body and health of hell and will have a remarkable and extremely positive impact on your days. Here are some lessons from his book that you can start working with.

Lesson # 1

Eat to preserve life. Foods and drinks feed life. For this reason, you must consider the act of feeding yourself as a supplement to life that should not be overlooked or abused. The stomach and the spleen receive the nutrients which, in turn, send the liquid to organs and viscera, as grass and trees grow by the Qi of the earth.

In other words, taking care of your stomach and paying attention to what you give it is of utmost importance to take care of the body. The ancestors always limited what they ate to avoid the excesses which destabilize the hormones and the thousands chemical reactions where the ultimate goal is to reach a balance, optimal functioning.

Nobody has ever eaten by accident. The ancients often said it: "The disease enters by the mouth and the disasters come out of it.". What you eat and drink must quench thirst and quell the hunger. Once these two goals are accomplished, you must stop. Control yourself and set limits.

Lesson # 2

Be grateful. Gratitude is the opposite of greed and envy, cures anger and resentment, encourages contentment and promotes moderation, restraint, and balance. Optimal health is what you deserve and what you owe to those around you. Be grateful to your parents and the very nature that gives you everything you need to stay alive. Neglecting your health is of the highest ingratitude to society and your parents who educate and support you.

Lesson # 3

One of the first principles of Yojokun is to avoid overexposure to elements or circumstances that could damage your body. There are two categories, inner desires, and external influences. Internal desires include food, drink, sex, sleep, talking too much, and the seven emotions such as joy, hate, anxiety, longing, pain, fear, and astonishment.

Negative external influences are the 4 dispositions of nature: wind, cold, heat and humidity. Being able to control one's inner desires is the true foundation of how to feed life. With a solid foundation, your strength will continually increase and you will be able to repel external influences. However, a lack of attention to your desires will weaken your health and leave you susceptible to external influences.

The essential elements to feed your Qi[4], are;
1. Eliminate hatred and desire.
2. Decrease grief and nostalgia.
3. Never disturb the spirit or the Qi.
4. Never sleep too much. The Qi does not circulate very well in a horizontal position for prolonged periods.
5. Never go to bed with your stomach full.
6. Never eat until saturated. Set limits. Never sit, lie down or stand too long. Move to move the Qi.

Lesson # 4

An old saying says, "The wise man treats before he gets sick." A little prevention helps to completely prevent diseases. Sun Tzu[5] said, "A man who uses his army effectively will not perform outstanding meritorious deeds. In other words, by using your resources properly, you will avoid big and dangerous battles. He also mentioned that the elders, skilled at defeating the enemy, were also the ones who would have defeated the most easily defeated by using and maximizing the most effective warfare

---

[4] The notion of qi evolves simultaneously on three levels; that of living beings, that of the structure of the universe and that of spirituality. By extension, the notion is also used to account for an effect of harmony, be it artistic, architectural or physical. The interpretation of qì in terms of energy remains peculiar to the West, because it never appears in the Chinese texts which remain, them, the idea of a breath or an essence. In this spiritual approach, the qì is at the origin of the universe and connects the beings and the things between them: "we do not possess the chi, we are the chi!" 6 It circulates inside the body by meridians that intersect all in the "center of energies" called "cinnabar field", tanden in Japan and dāntián in China. He is present in all the manifestations of nature.

[5] The Author of the military strategy book: The Art of War. The main idea of his work is that the objective of the war is to force the enemy to abandon the struggle, including without combat, thanks to cunning, espionage and great mobility: it is therefore a question of adapt to the strategy of the opponent to ensure victory at a lower cost.

techniques, often even before setting foot on the battlefield.

This is exactly how one should use Yojokun's principles, commit to being victorious before the battle begins.

Lesson 5

One day at a time is the golden rule. Be attentive to the present moment. Live and experience one day at a time. By using common sense from morning till night, you will not make mistakes, suffer little or any damage, and cause no disaster in your lifetime. Live for this day, she prepares you for the next.

CHAPTER 4

NUTRITION

Without having the proper plan, especially adding a few strength and conditioning sessions on top of your BJJ sessions, you will have to put as much attention in your nutrition as you do about rolling.

My goal for this section is to give you all the necessary tools to be able to create simple habits (nutritionally speaking) based on your individual needs. In my opinion, creating positive habits is the most important aspect of the game as its how you will rest and regenerate, getting ready physically for the next sessions, 10x10, shark tanks or for the big step, competition.

We have seen incredible success stories from people who started training BJJ. I, myself, underwent an incredible change. I lowered my body fat from more than 20% to now a comfortable 10% in just about 6 months. It even got me noticed by Men's Health magazine, for which they interviewed me on how I did it. Don't forget, I'm a seasoned trainer and trainee. I have been training for more than 30 years. Lack of motivation caught up to me and I needed a change of pace. From a young age, martial arts were a part of me. I did Aikido, judo, Japanese traditional JuJitsu, and kickboxing but with a successful business and family, I found it harder to find more time and especially, motivation. I help people all day, everyday to become better versions of themselves, but couldn't find the little motivation I needed to help myself. That's when Jits came in and got back in the game very fast.

Don't get this wrong, the change of shape can not only be attributed to rolling hard and training like a mad man. 80%, if not more, came from nutrition.

You need to realize that you need to feed the machine. You can't be training 3-4 times a week without thinking about eating cleaner and, wait for it…without eating more!! To lose weight, the answer is not always to eat less. Let me explain.

Your metabolism is responsible for 3 things. To convert food into energy for your cells, the conversion of food/fuel to building blocks for proteins, lipids, and carbohydrates, and the elimination of wastes. The word metabolism can also refer to the sum of all chemical reactions that occur in living organisms, including digestion and the transport of substances into and between different cells[iv].

So your metabolism needs nutrients to function. Up until now, no big news or else, you wouldn't be able to read this. We also need to know the Basal metabolic rate, which is what the minimum requirement of what our body needs to function at rest, to keep the vital functions running such as breathing, circulation, body temperature, cell growth and repair, brain and nerve function and some muscle functions. Basal metabolic rate (BMR) affects the rate that a person burns calories and ultimately whether that individual maintains, gains, or loses weight. The basal metabolic rate accounts for about 60 to 75% of the daily calorie expenditure by individuals. It is influenced by several factors and starts declining after age 20 by 1-2 % per decade due to the loss of lean tissue[v], although the variability between individuals is high[vi].

Another simple way to lose muscle mass and to age faster is to burn more calories than we can ingest, as in a lot more. Most people fail their new years' resolutions because of this simple fact. They usually eat about 3 meals a day, and not the so-called balanced meal (protein, carbs, and fat) as proposed by almost any nutritionist. A toast in the morning, a nice light salad for lunch and one hell of a dinner at night. The problem is that they don't eat enough calories, especially since they want to succeed in their newfound resolution and want to shred the pounds off fast. On top of that, that big evening meal will make them sleep on a full stomach, messing up their sleep patterns.

I hate to count calories, as they are not all equal. But for the sake of understanding the basic principle of eating to live, this is the best way to explain one of the most basic principles in performance nutrition. Your basal metabolic rate is calculated with the Harris-Benedict formula as follows;

Men

BMR = (10 × weight in kg) + (6.25 × height in cm) - (5 × age in years) + 5

Woman

$$BMR = (10 \times \text{weight in kg}) + (6.25 \times \text{height in cm}) - (5 \times \text{age in years}) - 161$$

This is basically the amount of calories you burn at rest, doing nothing, like the basic minimum you are required to live and for normal cell and organ functions.

So for a 35-year-old male of 175 pounds at 68 inches, his BMI would be of about 1700 calories a day.

Now, for daily caloric needs, we also have to add exercising and physical work if it is the case. So let's say that that same male workouts about 4 times a week, we would have to multiply by 1.55 his BMI, adding another 1000 calories a day required to meet his needs. So he needs about 2700 calories a day for optimal cognitive and physiological functions, to recuperate, regenerate and make sure he is ready to attack the following days.

The following table enables the calculation of the recommended daily kilocalorie intake to maintain current weight[vii].

Little to no exercise Daily kilocalories needed = BMR x 1.2
Light exercise (1–3 days per week) = BMR x 1.375
Moderate exercise (3–5 days per week) = BMR x 1.55
Heavy exercise (6–7 days per week)= BMR x 1.725
Very heavy exercise (twice per day, extra heavy workouts)= BMR x 1.9

Like many, thinking that adding some type of exercise in their daily routine would only make them lose weight is somewhat of a mistake. The outcome can vary from one individual to another. Counting calories as well.

The rule of thumb to lose weight is to have a slight deficit in calories. A 300 to 500 calories deficit is recommended for an individual to lose weight, but calories are not the only health marker you have to keep in check and so is the weight on the scale.

You could lose weight but not body fat, which is what your main goal should be. You could stay at the same weight on the scale but lose a great deal of body fat and gain lean muscle mass at the same time. You can gain weight on the scale and still lose some bodyfat and the worst outcome is also possible, like losing muscle mass and gaining fat, which still wouldn't even show on the scale. The lesson here is to not only focus on the scale.

As a strength and conditioning professional, I would suggest that you get someone to do your body fatt as soon as you start. It also goes without saying that you should consult your physician before trying any type of physical activity.

Nutrition is about eating to fuel the body, it always has been the goal. Until we have found ways to make food faster and in large quantity, that's when things got messed up. TV dinners, pizza pockets, and fast food are killing our health. Then you see some genetic freaks who can eat almost anything and show better abs than any fitness know it all on Instagram. They say that they can eat anything they want and get away with it. Maybe. However, you might be able to out-train a bad diet, but it is only a matter of time before it catches up to you.

Furthermore, there are also those who run a very strict regimen and swear by it. They count every single calorie they can find. They even count yours and scold you on it. That is a problem since counting calories is a big waste of time.

The problem with calorie Counting

I have often written articles where I dared to touch the subject of the famous calories. I even had to calculate the calories of some meals in some articles and as expected, the comments from the keyboard soldiers quickly came in. I was the worst of the incompetents and I had to withdraw from the coaching profession because I supposedly miscalculated the calories of meals by omitting some 50 calories here and there. In my opinion, trying to fight the soldiers of calories is a lost cause.

Often, reminding of an obsessive disorder, calculating the exact amount they eat gives them a sense of security because they believe they can control the nutrition aspect of their lives. The problem is not only that they believe they control what they eat, but also the energy expenditure matches the calories ingested, which is not quite applicable, the reality is completely different.

Calories will always be a very mixed debate, because, in some people, the day is dedicated, for the most part, to calculate the calories of their meals and sometimes even that of others ... to educate they say.

Improving our health and well-being is, without a doubt, very important. When we think of exercise and all we eat as the only way to lose weight, or worse yet, a punishment for weight gain instead of some bigger goals, we end up sabotaging our efforts to try to create a healthier way of life.

The advice that has been circulating for moons is to cut about 100 calories a day in order to lose 10 lbs over a year. The math behind this logic is that 1 lb of fat equals 3500 calories, so necessarily 100 calories a day for a duration of 365 days will give a total of 10 pounds lost.

This simplistic theory is far from reality. After a short while dieting and a significant weight loss, the system will adjust by lowering the metabolic rate in order to save on its energy expenditure, enough to balance the incoming energy reduction. For those who reduce their weight, the energy expenditure is decreased after a certain time, so the deficit returns to zero after a few weeks.

It must also be remembered that this is only an average. Physiological, genetic and intestinal flora differences have a huge influence on weight loss from the same calorific deficit. Finally, no one can calculate exactly how to cut 100 calories, let alone keep this accuracy over extended periods. This " illusion " nurtures the inner nerve and rational thinking, but remember that getting exact numbers is virtually impossible.

The information on the labels looks accurate, 150 calories for 6 ounces seem, actually, very accurate, but it's, in fact, only an approximation of what a person can draw as energy. We can use that energy for physical activity or turn it into fat, but it does not stop there. Foods can also be excreted because they have not been well digested and/or absorbed. Energy expenditure differs depending on the individual's corpulence, the ratio between muscle and fat can vary by more than 250 calories between two almost identical individualsviii.

Nobody counts calories for pleasure, the goal will always be to lose weight through a caloric deficit and principles belonging to a certain type of diet. We must also think of those who influence the message. Low-calorie foods give the illusion of diet and control. These are, in my opinion, calories well hidden and useless for our bodies.

Even though the industry is widely criticized for the fact that junk food is directly linked to a growing rate of obesity, we still have to be realistic and understand that if the industry continues to produce this type of food in industrial quantities, it's just because people ask for it and buy it. They try to soften the blame by justifying that with a balanced diet, it is not 'serious' to eat junk foods, you just do not exceed your calories. They also try to point out the lack of will and discipline of people who suffer from health problems due to obesity and all the related problems. On the other hand, they do not mention the constant effort of the industry and the fundingix of ads and targeted ads that challenge those who are trying to make a difference or are trying to pay attention to their health.

In 1965, the majority of meals were prepared at home, mostly by women, unlike today where 2/3 of meals are not eaten at home and just over half prepare their meals.

If you still doubt it, for those who start training and have never read my blogs, several articles support the benefits of training, if only by this meta-analysis that confirms that out of 100,000 people, physically fit people are 42% less likely to die prematurelyx. So following being active decreases your chances of dying faster by almost half. You want even more specific? Every improvement in your time or speed of a mile is associated with a 22.6% reduction in your chances of premature deathxi.

The key remains, without a doubt, our habits. We take certain habits to achieve a particular goal, but once the goal is achieved, good habits must remain. The more we practice these new habits, the more they will become an automatism and dictate our behavior. For behavior to become a habit, it must be repeated in the same context and for the same reasons on a regular basis and a reward must be attached to it. Research tells us that automating a habit can take between 18 and 254 days, the average being 66 days. Those who repeated the habit on a daily basis were able to succeed more quickly.

So to get out of the dogmas of controlled diets, eat conscientiously. Once you recognize certain triggers, you just have to put a hurdle to make this bad habit more difficult to practice. Like those who decide to stop smoking, but keep some cigarettes in the house... Not a very good way to stop the bad habit of smoking.

In this case, and as with every person who practices a restricted diet, recognizing the elements that lead to cheating and eating more than necessary will greatly assist the process and make the task less difficult. Counting calories is not a problem as such, it remains to be seen why some do it and why are they seeking such control? If we practiced this simple habit, that is, eat the right foods when we are hungry and stop to satiety, overweight would be virtually non-existent. A diet should never be restrictive. The word diet should not exist, point: this is what the media, stress, society, and purpose related to the desire for perfection revealed to us.

Now let's get back to our regular program…

Nutritionally speaking, great habits start by **having the minimum requirement of protein.** This is the number one habit I believe can dramatically change your shape and overall health.

Now, I hope you didn't get into the bandwagon of "meat can kill you" propaganda. All to begin with this famous research linking meat and premature death. Several arguments surfaced proving this imprecise and incomplete search.

-Here's how the research was conducted.

The firm responsible for leading the research is specialized in hazard identification, not risk assessment. Their mandate is not to tell us how important an item can cause cancer, but only if it can cause it or not. Take a banana peel. It can certainly cause accidents - but in practice, this does not happen very often and the injuries it can cause are usually not as serious as, for example, a car accident. But under a hazard identification system like IARC, "banana peel" and "car accidents" would fall under the same category - both can certainly cause accidents.

-Participants should have passed a basic examination battery, blood pressure, weight, size, cholesterol, etc. and be followed for several years. Processed meat-eaters were much less active, had a higher BMI, were three times more likely to smoke and almost twice as likely to have diabetes.

A bad habit is often followed by others, as much as good habits are always accompanied by others as well. A healthy person usually does not eat or little processed meats. Those who eat processed meats are often the ones who are madly out of a healthy diet, along with several other bad habits to make it worse.

"Do you remember what you ate last Friday?" More so what you ate a month or a year ago? These are the kinds of questions they had to answer.

Search a little and you will find a significant number of shortcomings of this research. Eat quality meat and vary the kinds. There is a lot more you can eat than beef and Chicken. Turkey, wild boar, deer, ostrich, bison, etc. These should be part of your meat inventory. More variety will bring more spice to your diet.

For us athletes, we require a minimum because of our more active lifestyle. We need protein to rebuild muscle tissue, to recover faster and boost our cognitive abilities and immune system.

The baseline requirement for guys should be around 1 to 1.5 g protein/kg per day and girls, .8 to 1.2 g protein/kg per day. Current recommendations for protein intakes during weight loss in athletes are set at 1.6-2.4g protein/kg/d[xii]. However, the severity of the caloric deficit and type and training intensity performed will influence at what end of this range athletes choose to be at.

Why most trainers and I are so adamant about eating protein? Here are a few reasons why;

- Studies show that protein is by far the most filling. It helps you feel more full — with less food[xiii]. This is partly because protein reduces your level of the hunger hormone ghrelin. It also boosts the levels of peptide YY, a hormone that makes you feel full [xiv].

- Protein is a building block to build and preserve your hard-earned muscles.

- People who eat more protein tend to maintain bone mass better as they age and have a much lower risk of osteoporosis and fractures[xv].

- High protein intake may boost your metabolism significantly, helping you burn more calories throughout the day.

- Protein can help your body repair after it has been injured. This makes perfect sense, as it forms the main building blocks of your tissues and organs. Numerous studies demonstrate that eating more protein after an injury can help speed up recovery[xvi]

- Eating more protein may reduce cravings and desire for late-night snacking. Merely having a high-protein breakfast may have a powerful effect. Which leads me to my next point.

I am a big believer in eating **a big ol' breakfast**. However, my definition might be a little different than a bowl of fruit loops or captain crunch.

Breakfast time is seen as the most important meal of the day and for good reasons. The first thing you eat in the morning has been known to have a huge impact on the rest of your day, your productivity and has a great influence on your body composition.

Every single time I ask a new client how is their breakfast, the answer is 99% of the time "Heathy", so they say. However, it might not be their fault. In reality, it is not what we were led to believe. The modern breakfast consists of cereal products, fruit juices, "pseudo Healthy ' low fat spread, toast, and coffee. Most of us know very well that this kind of breakfast is not what it should be, but simply an adaptation of false studies, beliefs, and lobbying by food industry, an adaptation that fits our daily stress and lack of time in the morning. Food is the first line of defense to support the proper functioning of the human body, it is not surprising that conditions directly related to nutrition such as diabetes, cardiovascular disease, and hypertension have reached skyrocketing levels. More meds and/or development of new drugs do not address the root of the problems, which are often nutritional habits.

A great breakfast will influence several aspects of your day, such as better work performance, more energy during your workouts, your mood, and quality time with your children after a hard day of work. Just the simple fact of having a nutrient-dense breakfast instead of the sugar boosted one will help you improve your body composition without great struggle. Several studies prove it.

There is a great debate about the best method to lose fat, workout on an empty stomach in the morning or after a good breakfast? Here is one for fans of fasted cardio.

Two groups of young men were tested by measuring their oxygen consumption rate (VO2) and respiratory quotient (RQ) post-workout (cardio training at 65% MHR) with breakfast and fasting. Each group had the same quantity and quality of food for the next 24 hours. The breakfast group had the largest increase in VO2 and QR, indicating greater fat oxidation and there was a significant difference between the two groups in the 24 hours following exercise. The author concluded that to train on an empty stomach does not increase fat oxidation, but a light meal before training will maximize your results.

The next question would be when is a good time to eat before rolling? There might be two issues here, one would be digestion and how big of a meal. If you already have issues with digestion, I would suggest that you eat at least 2-3 hours before rolling, with a meal easy to digest. Low fat, lean protein, and veggies. The higher the fat content, the longer it will take to digest.

Motivation influences much of our day. We are frequently asked how to improve people's motivation, whether for training, cheating (food-wise), etc. Believe it or not, your breakfast has a lot to do with it when it is time to kick ass. Researchers from The University of Missouri have examined the benefits of a high protein breakfast on obese young girls or overweight in late adolescence. They studied the hormonal and neural effects of a high protein breakfast on appetite during the day, satiety, motivation and the need to reward themselves with food. The first group had lunch with lunch 350 kcal, cereal (13 grams of protein) and a second group with the same number of Kcal but consists of eggs and beef. After only six days, they concluded that only the group with high protein breakfast had a significant (positive) difference in satiety and greater motivation.

Now, what should be the best options for a decent breakfast knowing all we know now? Keep in mind that a great breakfast should allow you to burn fat, ensure optimal mental acuity and ideal blood sugar throughout the day. A breakfast rich in nutrients, such as a source of animal protein or eggs, a small serving of fruit (such as berries or grapes) and a small amount of nuts will assure you the best results. It goes without saying that the quality of the meat should be organic sourced and free-range. It is essential to avoid sources of processed meats like luncheon meats/cold cuts (deli), which are a major source of nitrate and also what they can't use with regular cuts of meat, such as cartilage, tendons, fat, etc. It is for this reason that they write down 15% protein on the packaging of what looks like a big ball of meat...

Here are some examples of breakfast:

1. Patties of minced meat, a handful of pine nuts, 1 cup raspberries

2. 1-2 eggs over easy on the steak of choices, chopped spinach, almonds

3. Scrambled eggs with spinach, avocado, tomatoes, some macadamia nuts

4. 3 eggs over easy on sliced chicken breast with blackberries and Brazil nuts.

5. Omelet with cheddar (non-pasteurized milk), and asparagus with blueberry and cashews

6. Protein powder, eggs and coconut flour (pancake style) with almond butter.

7. A portion of plain Greek yogurt 2% or more, with fruits, 1 egg and a serving of veggies.

Of course, your breakfast is not your entire diet, however, it is probably the most misunderstood meal of the day. The human body is designed to eat in the morning and especially to eat nutritious foods that will not adversely affect its performance. As you can see from our recipe ideas, there are several good ways to start your day.

With the breakfast taken care of, the rest of your day should go smoothly. As long as you can reach your protein goal as you read earlier and tons of veggies along with it, your body composition and recuperation will thank you for it.

It doesn't have to be very complicated.

Another question I get often is portion size. Now, I'm not into measuring even if it looks badass and dedicated, I don't and most of my clients don't have time to measure whatever they eat, three times a day. What I learned throughout the years is how to eyeball it.

1 serving size of protein, all meats (anything that was alive before) is about the thickness and size of the palm of your hand. For him, I recommend two serving sizes and her, 1 serving.

Serving size of veggies is as big as your fist. Again, I would recommend 2 servings for a man and 1 for her.

For carbs like starches, fruits, and grains, 2 cupped hands is good enough for him and 1 cupped hand for her.

For fat intakes, such as grains, oils, avocados, butter and nut-butters, 2 thumb-sized for him and 1 for her.

Now that we got all the numbers down and that you can start to create your plan, let me throw you a curveball. As you start to change, as you start to roll and get accustomed to the game, you will learn to save energy. The more years you get under your belt, the better you become at it, does that make sense?

The same goes for those who run marathons. You become more efficient at saving energy and more efficient at the activity itself. So the fact of the matter is that you probably will have to adjust everything, your nutrition, your workouts, constantly. Nutritionally speaking, your body will change and the absolute truth is this, your body will constantly be trying to balance things out. Which is why I hate the word diet.

It eradicates the principle of "healthy eating". Dieting negatively affects your health because people fail to recognize when they are actually hungry, hence making them more vulnerable to eat their emotions and/or have episodes of binge eating. Researchxvii has shown that there is no difference between losing weight and gaining it back and maintaining a slightly elevated weight while staying healthy.

Enter the principle of the defended weight.

Your body adapts to a given weight and can fluctuate between 10-15 lbs, which is a sort of thermostat that regulates the balance between energy in/energy out. He defines the weight range as the norm. However, once he reaches the lower or higher end, symptoms start showing up. The lower end will leave you cold and always hungry with no energy and those who will eat without being hungry will lean towards the higher end of the norm.

It's easy to make a house colder by opening up a window but it won't change the temperature setting on the thermostat. The system will try to bring up the temperature by activating the heaters to bring up the temperature to its initial setting. In this case, our brain has the same purpose as the thermostat. On a diet, it will do everything in its powers to go back to its defended weight.

Hold on now, it doesn't mean that you should not worry when in the higher end of your defended weight. If you stay too long in the higher range, your brain will see it as the new norm. Unfortunately, we can't say the same for the lower range. The reason why it is so hard to keep the weight off is that your body will also do everything in its power to stay in the mid-range, where it is the most comfortable.

So it will take your body a lot longer to adapt to the lower range than to the stay in the higher range. The trick is to do it the healthy way. Slow and steady.

Metabolic Clean-Up

Before we go on, some might want to gain weight or lose weight, which is fine. In spite of this, one of the best things to do for your body is what I call a little metabolic cleanup. We often get caught up in diets that make us eat 5 or six times a day, or that we are stuck eating the same foods over and over again. We often lean towards the food that makes us feel good, to alleviate stress. We love to eat because it tastes good. I'm all good for that but it has taken a very steep turn in the past 50 years. We lost touch with what is truly the foundation of great nutrition. We should eat to live, not the other way around. We stopped listening to our instinct. We eat until we explode. For those in the training world, we learned quickly that skipping meals is catabolic, we start losing our hard-earned muscle mass. Typical bodybuilding diets force us to eat 5 or 6 meals a day, forcing our digestion to work non stop, which is in my opinion, detrimental to our health if done continuously.

The metabolic clean up is fairly simple and not something I invented. It's just pure logic. You often see it in books or specialized 12 weeks program. The start the first few weeks with the basics and then they add on to it. The main goal is to give a break to the digestive system and reset the insulin response.

You basically eat the minimum caloric and nutrient requirement in a day. You will essentially eat 3 simple meals in a day at about 4 to 5 hours interval between each meal. You have to cut down on all simple sugar, dairy products, and all man-made food. Think of it as if you were stuck in a cabin in the woods and stuck eating with whatever nature and your garden would provide. You will be eating anything that your body was made to digest easily. We were genetically designed as omnivores. Meat, veggies, fruits, nuts, or anything that nature can provide. Nothing that comes in boxes and cans.

It seems easy on paper, but for those who are used to eat every 2 to 3 hours will be in for a ride. Your body has some kind of signal, which triggers insulin to break down sugar (very vulgar way to explain) and that's why some people can stop eating. Cortisol is the main stress hormone and the body gets also rid of it with insulin. So imagine a stressful day with lots of food in it. Disturbed digestion and metabolic stress for days on end.

Eating less resets this signal and helps normalize blood sugar. Healthier blood sugar means a lot of benefits all around. The fat loss assured, and improved glycogen storage. In other words, easier to gain lean muscle mass while still losing some unwanted fat mass. You will also get rid of these late-night cravings. The first few days, however, some might go through hell.

Energy levels may drop, you'll probably feel a little out of it, unfocused and a little brain fog. This is your body cleaning up. The first thing you'll notice after a few days is your mind getting sharper. Another great advantage is the improvement in sleep quality. Deeper and more restful sleep. The other great benefit is the control you have over your satiety. You will realize when you are full and better manage your portion sizes. Nonetheless, you will quickly see a difference in body composition. You will also see your energy levels change positively, with improved stamina.

THE PLAN

Now that we have cleared up what needs to be done in order to clean up your eating habits and have gone through the first metabolic cleanup, you can now take it a step further.

If you jump right at the end of the book, you'll find a list of macronutrients and a template where you can build and pick from to build your own plan.

The portion sizes are indicated and it gives an approximation of how much calories you'll be taking in, but as you know now, counting calories is not and will never be an exact science. With that being said, here is an example of how I would use this plan.

Losing weight

This may be for competition or just for health reasons. There are many ways you can lose weight, but the goal is to lose fat. In order to do so, you need to create a slight deficit as explained previously. Many types of diets can bring you decent results. But before you dive into one of them, try the K.I.S.S. principle, keep it simple stupid. Did you cut out all the refined carbs? All the junk and soft drinks? By taking out all sources of simple sugars from your diet, half the job is done and it will probably show faster than you ever thought it would. All you need is a little willpower.

I usually tell people to do a detox for a maximum of 3 weeks, but not the traditional over the counter detox kits that you would buy at the pharmacy. Detox as in "take out all the man-made food out of your house" type of 3 weeks. Anything that comes in a box, or that you have to mix up together and bake for it to be eaten. If it doesn't fly, swim, run, crawl, or not green, you don't eat it. It's as simple as that.

What we have failed to do in the past few 100 years is to learn how to listen to our bodies. Our instinct and energy expenditure dictate to us how we should eat. I'm sure that you feel like some days, you are not that hungry and other days you could eat everything. Now, unfortunately, because we have everything at almost arms reach, eating for the sake of taste has lead us to this obesity pandemic. In our case, training days should have more meals than on rest days, the logic is there. We obviously spend less energy on rest days than on rolling and training days. Start by implementing these few tips first and let everything fall into place slowly. Rome was not built in one day.

Gaining weight

If you think that it is easier to gain weight than to lose it, you might be in for a ride. Again, gaining weight should be aimed at gaining lean muscle mass. Eating more does not actually mean gaining lean tissue, it often comes with fat gains, depending on what you eat obviously. So trying to gain weight does not mean that you can eat freely anything you want. It could bring serious issues and may slow you down.

Depending on where you are body composition wise, if you are higher than 12%, I would suggest that you bring down your bodyfat lower than 12% before you start thinking of gaining muscle mass as a unique goal. The thing is that you will probably gain muscle mass as you try to lose fat. Yes, both are possible at the same time. A higher percentage of fat means that your body is battling some inflammation due to poor glycogen metabolism, which makes it more difficult to gain lean muscle. Fat tissue increases aromatase, which turns testosterone into estrogen. We don't want more estrogen boys. By eating well, you keep your liver clean and well for healthy fat and estrogen metabolism. In other words, it converts it and excretes it outside the body. The liver is our Captain America, kicks out the bad guy if you treat him well.

For those who want to gain weight aka muscle, increasing protein intake is the best way to go. Instead of the baseline, go more on the 1.5 to 2.0gr/kg/d and girls would be 1 to 1.5gr/kg/d.

Now, why would you want to gain lean muscle mass? Isn't it just the weight on the scale that is important? Is it going to make me slower on the mats? I just have to eat and I'll gain lean muscle mass. Unfortunately, it doesn't work that way.

Let's just say that you would want to make weight for a given category, Going up or down the scale is always a challenge, especially going up. Losing weight, depending on body composition, is always tricky. Exception made for UFC fights, where they only fight once in the card, I wouldn't suggest the severe weight cuts they go through for BJJ competition. You might have 2 to 5 fights in one category in the span of an hour, which is insane energy-wise. So getting ready to fight at a given weight a few weeks before is the best to get prepared. The more you roll at that weight, more comfortable you become. Drastic weight changes are not recommended since it takes a toll on the nervous and muscular system and adaptation takes a bit of time to get accustomed to.

Gaining weight however, takes time and is often just a matter of hydration and proper glycogen storage.

Competition

For those trying their hands at the competition, the approach in BJJ is not the same as other fighting sports. We often see M.M.A. fighters cutting crazy amounts of weight before the big fight night. They train at a given weight for a few months, in already great shape and lean as they can be, but the weigh-in requires them to still be 10lbs, often 20 lbs under what they are used to train and fight at. Their weigh-in is the night before, so they have a good 24 hours to gain back the weight they lost.

The drastic measures and length some of them go through to lose the weight are very drastic and often dangerous. The big issue is dehydration, where they lose lots of water weight. Some of them wear plastic suits and spend hours in saunas and hot baths to shed excess water weight. This practice has been around for a while and a few died from it. This is not to be taken lightly and has to be done under the supervision of professionals.

For BJJ competition, however, the game is completely different. Depending on your level and the organizational bodies, the fight could last between 5 and 8-10 minutes. Depending on your weight brackets, you could fight only 3 times and as much as 5 or 6 fights in the span of one hour.

Also, the weigh-in is done in the morning or right before the fight, but again, it all depends on the organization you are fighting in.

Imagine the implication, the planning behind this crucial day. First and foremost, you fight the same day of the weight. Unlike the MMA fights, you can't eat that much before the fight, maybe 1 or 2 light meals. The fight is often delayed, so you can't really plan a meal around the fight.

My best advice for BJJ competition would be to be at fighting weight or lower a week or two before the competition. Those two weeks prior to the competition are crucial. You are supposed to roll more, work on your plan (more of this in the special section on psychological warfare) and since you should be a little lighter a few days before due to all the intense competition drilling and rolling sessions, you'll be able to eat comfortably without starving to death and have a full head on your shoulders, ready and focused.

Moreover, the tougher sessions will call for more calories, so don't think that you'll have to cut down like crazy to lose the excess weight. More often than not people who cut too much calories while training more, end up in a few bad scenarios. They can't lose a pound, they feel sluggish and lose a lot of strength while some can gain fat!

Your first competition will be the testing ground for all these variables. This is where it is important to have a written plan. You don't go into your first competition head-on, expecting to win. There is always the possibility, but it is much more a learning experience than anything else. Write down as much as you can about your preparation, learn from it and on to the next one.

CHAPTER 5

DECONSTRUCTING JITS

To better understand the needs of any sports, I have to de-assemble it, put it into puzzle pieces. I do the same with the athlete in front of me. As I put all the pieces back together, I create the perfect program for the goals in mind.

Understanding the sport's needs and how to bring all the intricate details into a given program is as crucial as understanding the muscle imbalances of the athlete. Only then you will know what to include in the program to make the body perform at its best when the time has come.

What follows are the main moves and important aspects of Brazilian JiuJitsu. As you already know, there are some elements of wrestling, grappling, and even boxing. My intent for this chapter is to go into greater detail of what, when and where you need to focus on because if you understand those details well, the better you'll be able to design and incorporate the proper exercises to correct muscle imbalances and issues. You'll also get a view from both sides. As you'll learn how to improve joint and muscle integrity, it is as important to know what can go to shit with possible risks of injuries.

For **self-defense**, standing or ground striking is essential. Knowing the proper mechanics and how to train them gives you the edge, as much as knowing when to back the fuck up. Then there are headlocks and clinch/holds.

The clinch/collar tie/snap down and jab.

In no gi, there are far less grips and possible take downs so grips and positional dominance have to be strong and the core plays an even game, if not more due to the speed of the no Gi game.

To establish dominance, controlling the head of the opponent is the advantage. Control the head and the body will follow. The infamous collar tie/neck-tie/clinch can deter the attention of your opponent for a fraction of seconds if you "slap" it hard enough and while being able to get ready for the snap-down. I'm not talking of an overhead karate chop, see it as some type of a jab with a clamp at the end. The collar tie can lead to a snap down, guillotine, ankle pick, single-leg, throws, etc…Which is why that little fraction of a second can have a huge impact.

If you understand and execute the jab well, you'll make this technique very efficient. The boxing jab has little to do with the strength of the arm. It is like a whip-crack, produced by a ripple in the material of the whip traveling towards the tip, rapidly escalating in speed until it breaches the famous bullwhip sound. Visualize the jab the same. The back leg is pushing you forward and the chain of movement, from the legs, the core and shoulder transfer all the energy on to the extension on the arm (your fist) similar to the whip.   As the jab's purpose is to mainly distance the opponent, the clinch's purpose is to close in, control his posture and block further attacks. As you throw the jab or close in for the clinch, the muscles of the posterior chain are the main subjects.

When we talk about the posterior chain, it involves and starts from all the little stability sensors and small muscles in the foot, which initiates the drive forward, firing up the calf muscles. Than the quadriceps and buttocks extend the knee of the back leg driving the explosiveness of the drive forward. The front leg engages the hamstring, pulling the body forward.

The same goes when you establish your grips in Gi and no Gi, especially if you want to grab the neck or lapel. Make it explosive. The Little slap given as you grab the neck should feel like a small concussion. Hey, don't try to be nice? Dominate.

Obviously, having a great and strong neck is best, for any type of takedowns, which is where a lot of injuries happen. Low back, knees and neck strains are often the result of bad falls. For Uke, defending grips and the snap-down is the task at hand and maybe countering the shoot for the single or double leg by sprawling. Again, the posterior chain (hamstring, buttocks and low back) are to be engaged to sprawl and blocking the attempt for the takedown. The core, low back, abs and upper body are controlling Tori's upper body while the legs and hips are pushing his upper body down.

Takedowns

Double leg, single leg or **ankle pick**, etc. The main issue, structurally speaking, is that you have to be careful about your neck, and your knees.

Depending on how you land after the double or single leg, your neck will probably take some part of the fall, and then you'll have to control or stabilize depending on where you land as well. Your head will have to push on the chest, all that while protecting your neck from guillotines or not to get swept back. Mind you, the one who is taken down also has some issues to deal with. Low back and neck which is some sort of double impact, standing and falling down on the mats. Some might even try to hold off the fall by trying to extend an arm back to absorb some of the fall, which often results in some sort of shoulder problems afterward.

As you shoot for a single leg or ankle pick, your knee might drop on the floor. There is also the possibility to wrap the other leg by dropping the knee on the floor behind a leg to block and make the opponent fall.

Knee functionality is crucial since as you fall, you never really know how and where you will land, which is why the importance of being able to fully bend the knee without any discomfort.

Knee problems are amongst the most common issues. Lack of proper strength training for the lower body, all across the weight lifting community is very common. In fight sports, most think that lifting weights, especially for lower body will impair their speed, which couldn't be further from the truth.

« You don't need to train your legs a lot for MMA or grappling sports » « gaining or training for strength will impair your flexibility » « Flexing your knees more than 90 degrees (squat below parallel) is bad for your knees »

Wrong! Maybe those are the reasons why knees are the most injured in any given sports. The lack of good, logical information and the abundance of bullshit training available on the net is mind-boggling.

Your knee is biomechanically made to bend more than 90 degrees. In fact, you should be able to squat down until your hamstring touches your calf. You can't? Yes, it's probably a flexibility problem, coming from the ankle, the quad, the hip or lower back. See the lack of flexibility as a way to protect the joints. Your lack of flexibility did not cause a problem. A problem (nutritional or structural) or an injury caused your lack of flexibility.

Most of the knees and backs injuries have two things in common, a strength discrepancy and a weakness in the chain. When you train for sports, training like a bodybuilder has some benefits but if it's all you do, you miss the big picture. The body moves as a whole.

The knee needs a structural balance. It starts from the foot and ankle, all the little intricate muscles are there to signal the nervous system what and how to fire up the posterior chain, the hips, the core.

As in a chain of command, the generals give all the special forces soldiers their given task to be ready for war, but what if one of the teams can't do their tasks? A big mess somewhere or, someone has to do the job for them.

So gaining strength is a no brainer. Strong and healthy knees will save you from being taken out of your favorite sports indefinitely.

Let's take the butterfly guard as a great example of complete knee flexion. Especially the defense, which is to bring the heel of the opponent to his butt, where you completely take out the strength of his leg and control most of it to pass.

Let's reverse the roles, you are the one applying the butterfly, going for the sweep, you'll have to load shift the opponent onto you to apply the sweep right? Now add a heavier opponent to the mix and one little slip or torque at the wrong angle could mean a snap or a sweep. We are told not to use the strength of our legs and if we load the weight correctly, we can sweep almost every type of opponent, in a perfect world. I would rather be safer than sorry and make sure my knees are up to par.

While looking at all knee angles, we can conclude that maximum knee flexion is optimal. It is a matter of flexibility and joint function. A variety of methods are useful, such as eccentric, concentric as well as isometric strength.

Now let's grasp another scenario. You get into comp class and you are faced with a new white belt. What you don't know is that he has some wrestling under his belt and a black belt in Judo!!! Gets his grips and next thing you know you are getting thrown faster than you can land one grip.

Brake falls are part of the game, which the upper body is "usually" the first thing that absorbs the fall but unfortunately, not all falls are the same. When the heel or hips touchdown first, it sends a shock wave to the extremities. If the knee is not strong enough, injuries or strains are often the results.

The four main ligaments in the knee are;

Anterior cruciate ligament (ACL) - The ligament that controls rotation and forward movement of the tibia.
Posterior cruciate ligament (PCL) - The ligament that controls the backward movement of the tibia.
Medial collateral ligament (MCL) - The ligament that gives stability to the inner knee.
Lateral collateral ligament (LCL) - The ligament that gives stability to the outer knee.

As you can imagine, breaking fall puts a tremendous and weird pressure on the knee, where the hamstrings, adductors, quads and hip rotators fire to protect the articulations and absorb most of the shock wave. All these ligaments are there to protect and limit excessive posterior, sideways and anterior movement but the number one reason why you should train your hamstrings is that it limits the displacements and strain on the ACL, which is the most common knee injury.

Ground

Once you are on the ground, the game gets much tighter and yes, it's complicated. With obviously less risk of injuries, if you want to survive, strength might be your best friend. Strength is not only a matter of pushing off and trying to be like a spazzy new white belt. I'm talking about strength to get out of bad situations, side control, back takes, etc. Unfortunately, lack of strength makes the joint weaker, which is where you need some type of protection to at least, have time to tap without having to ice your elbows for a few days or figure a way out, makes sense right?

Bridge and roll

This famous way to get out of mount is efficient with someone who is not expecting it. When you have someone with experience on top of you, you might have to bridge him over a few times to get what you want. The problem is the roll. It doesn't always happen as textbook unfortunately and that is when the shit hits the fan and pulled muscles happen. Twisting of the spine is probably the worst injury that can happen since it can cripple you for a few days, and also, it has the ability to change your posture if you don't take care of it immediately. That is the number one reason why it is called the bridge and roll. You bridge first in order to offset their balance and then you roll. Failing to bridge will make you twist your spine with such unnecessary energy that you'll end up hurting something, most probably your spine and/or lower back.

This one is all about the posterior chain. Low back and hamstrings and a bit of quadriceps will take care of the push-off also called "the bridge".

Passing and holding guard

With so many varieties, it's hard to pinpoint something in particular. If you look at what is involved, knees, feet and/or hands, the extremities are the key players, holding off the knees, trying to shift and control the direction of the floor player.

For both, the core is greatly engaged, more so for the one trying to hold his guard.

Once you get them in your guard, adductors and the core are pulling them in, trying to establish grips or going for a sweep. If the psoas is tight or unable to perform at best, the lower back and hips will seize up, especially for those who never lifted before.

Leg locks, heel hooks, and toe holds

Leg locks are a whole other world. Like the great Dean Lister said; why would you ignore 50% of the body? Go back and read the knee section of the takedowns. Unfortunately, strong knees will save you...to a certain point. Learn to tap before you hear a snap.

Heel hooks are a little sneaky when viewed from the untrained eye since maximum damaged could be caused on the knee because of some torque applied on the heel and foot. In reality, it puts tremendous strain on the ACL and LCL and if you don't learn to tap early, you'll be out for a while. Unfortunately, you can't really do anything for tendons and ligaments, except eating well and giving them the nutrients they need to stay strong and healthy.

Kimura/Omoplata and Americana's

A bit like the leg locks, tapping is your best way out. You could get away by trying to come out, but maybe only in competition. In training, your training partner should get it locked up, then when you know you can't or just don't want to get out because let's face it, he shouldn't have gotten it in the first place, tap and reset, save your shoulder. It's training, not competition. It's not like do or die.

Training the shoulder girdle/scapular chain efficiently can also save you from a few days off of rolling. Remember that those locks are basically testing the limit of the joints' range of motion. So you are basically at the weakest portion of the shoulder's strength curve for that given movement.

For both, the deltoid muscles, Subscapularis, Teres major and minor, supra and infraspinatus are all contracted and stretched or shortened to pain tolerance.

Having strong and healthy shoulders can give you a few seconds to get out and improve pain tolerance, I've even seen guys just lock the shoulder there and wait until the other guy starts another transition. Again, the stronger opponent, given equal abilities, will have the upper hand. In the first phase of the programs, we have included external rotation exercises to improve shoulder stability and strength.

The Omoplata is basically a kimura that you apply with your leg when they try to defend the arm bar from a closed guard. Which leads me to my next point.

The three brothers

This may be the first drill you'll be learning. The three brothers are basically a drill we do from a closed guard where one sub leads to another. Will not get into the details of the technique but you basically get an arm bar from closed guard, if he ends up pulling his arm out you sit up while having his other arm trapped in your lap and if he ends up again turning you over to go back into your guard, you get them into a triangle. The three brothers are all about leg positioning and hip placement.

Fluidity is the key. Someone that is trying to muscle its way through these 3 basic moves will only spend more energy than it is necessary. This is probably when you get to realize that strength is not a key player when trying to roll or submit, proper positioning and angles will lead the way. However, flexibility and stamina will be very helpful.

Arm bars

It's possible to survive an arm bar with the correct counter, but the pain can last forever. Elbow flexors are tested such as the forearm muscles and the long and short head of the biceps to counter the shearing force on the elbow. Learn to tap out before or be subjected to broken bones, injured muscles, tendons and ligaments and at the very least, a really sore limb the very next morning. The counter to one of the arm bar such as the one from Side mount is the "homer walk", where you walk counter-clockwise, only if the opponent doesn't control your leg. This counter not only puts great strain on the forearm, but shoulder mobility is tested to the max, which is why healthy and strong shoulders are best in this very sport.

The defense is a great demand on the arms and forearms when you might have to fight off legs pushing against your arms or just constant tension on your grip until it breaks and then bye bye elbow or he'll be forced to move into another position.

Guillotine and triangle chokes

I'm very sure that those who invented this killing machine during the French revolution would never have imagined that one of the most devastating submissions in MMA history would still carry its name. The mechanics of the guillotine is based on a single-arm applying a choke on its opponent. Where the rear-naked choke, which applies pressure on both sides of the neck where the carotid arteries are restricted, cutting the blood flow to the head, the guillotine also applies a neck crank, stretching the cervical area. Depending on the position, the head can be slightly turned sideways which stretches the trapezius down to the middle of the back and all the little intricate muscles of the neck that are not supposed to be stretched that way.

One of the ways to defend is to drop down the chin, which involves the neck flexors, the sternocleidomastoid, which you find on each side in front of the neck. You often have to absorb some of the torque and push off their hips, only if you catch them at the right moment. The guillotine though puts a strain on the neck extensors, mostly the levator scapulae (helps to lift your shoulders), Semispinalis Capitus (rotates the head and extends the ribs), splenius capitus (for head extension, as well as lateral flexion and rotation of the cervical spine) and trapezius muscles (move and support the arms and shoulders).

The same goes for triangles, from all positions. The problem with **triangles** is the angles you must take and the pulling some do on the lower leg. It can put a tremendous amount of stress on the meniscus and LCL ligament. Any activity that causes you to forcefully twist or rotate your knee, especially when putting your full weight on it, can lead to a torn meniscus.

Each of your knees has two menisci — C-shaped pieces of cartilage that act like a cushion between your shinbone and your thighbone. A torn meniscus causes pain, swelling, and stiffness. You also might feel a block to knee motion and have trouble extending your knee fullyxviii.

Neck injuries come in many varieties but unfortunately, there is no real remedy than rest and regeneration.

One common mistake I see with all neck injuries is the constant need to stretch the neck. Like all injuries, the muscle or tendon is already in a lot of stress, in inflammatory state. It's the same as if you are trying to stretch a bad that is already at its maximum tightness, all you are doing is putting more stress on the muscle. The common medical advice is to rest and immobilization. Icing is necessary for the first 24 hours to reduce swelling and following that, Heat might help as it brings in nutrients by increased blood flow and may help relax. Do not use heat treatments after activity, and do not use heat after an acute injury. Never use heat where swelling is involved because swelling is bleeding in the tissue, and heat just draws more blood to the area.

Cross side (attack and defend)

Controlling/defending and being caught in the cross side is most probably the hardest job to do. Usually, you get your points and move on, while being under, you need to get the hell out to not give the points.

Shrimping and bridging is the way to get out of arms way (pun intended) while your arms and legs try to create space when the opponent is trying to eliminate space. Bottom uses, in order of importance, arms and core, with the posterior chain that is working explosively to create distance to maybe pull a knee in to get closed guard or to grab a leg to gain half guard. Being able to sweep with the Gi or Turkish your way out of it requires a great understanding of leverage and the center of gravity. Proper positioning in transition or just before he comes into side control with a knee slide, there is the possible *Turkish get up*.

For the Turkish, core strength and coordination is important. Although it is a matter of proper positioning, you'll need strength since no Turkish in BJJ is the same. You basically do it against a force trying to bring you back down, unless he messed up along the way and has no clue about posting and limb positioning. Streetwise, the technical get up (top pictures), which is part of the Turkish, is a way of fending off or keeping the opponent at a distance since one arm stays in front. When finishing a sweep like the Ashi Garami, using the Turkish to get up helps controlling one leg while keeping the ability to safely get up and get the points.

You could practice the Turkish with a barbell or a dumbbell as shown in the middle pictures. Lying down while holding the weight as perpendicular as possible to the floor, crunch up and post on your elbow, continue the push-off on to your hand to bring the leg back and post on your knee. Get up by pushing the weight towards the ceiling. Reverse the steps to go back down. For BJJ, you don't have to get up, unless it's after a sweep to get points. Often, to get out of cross-side or mount, you might have to use the first portion of the Turkish, which is the initial push-off. Use a band to add a little more challenge. As the weight is constant with a barbell or dumbbell, the resistance increases exponentially with a band as you go up as shown in the lower right picture.

With as many positional varieties, controlling a cross side requires a great understanding of leverage and applying pressure at the right place and moment. The thing is that once you are applying cross side, your next move is an attack while trying to maintain and direct your opponent as best as possible towards the chosen sub.

On both sides, using too much strength to get out of control will only make matters worst. Learn to apply pressure or escape with proper leverage and technique. This is why, with any position, strength training is important so you can get out easier and use less energy to make that last-ditch effort.

Mount (attack and defend)

Maintaining mount is more of a rodeo ride, which involves the core and a good sense of balance and being in tune with your center of gravity until you decide to attack. You'll either have to post on your hands or sit back on your feet and engage.

Being stuck under is a job and a half and if the person is good on top, you'll have to be very creative and this is where posterior chain strength is of the utmost importance to get out and provoke some shit to happen or to break his transitions.

Still, the core is the main player as the extremities, arms, and legs, are working to gain control of a leg to move to half guard or trying to put them in your guard with the elbow knee escape.

Lower back/posterior chain is the weakest link with many, especially in the beginning. The first few months are very challenging and you can't really do anything but use strength. This is where the shit hits the fan, twisting, pushing in awkward ways using the back instead of pushing up with your legs and bridging properly.

Back

Again we see the core as a key player. If you are the one taking the back, closing in and eliminating the distance like an anaconda has to come from the core trying to pull in with the arms and feet.

Having your back taken, one of the few ways to get out is to put them on their back while putting pressure on their upper bodies while shifting your butt out to gain cross-side or reverse kase gatame. The posterior chain is engaged and the legs and core does most of the job by turning in while the arms keep the pressure on the opponents upper body.

CHAPTER 6

TRAINING

Like a lot of people, you probably skipped right away to this chapter since you want to get better, stronger, faster. I did the same when I browsed a few BJJ training books. What I failed to see is the lack of consideration of the experience of the trainee, you my friend.

So in order to fulfill what is the most crucial part of this book, your own personalized workout, you need to understand a few strength and conditioning laws. I will not delve into unnecessary notions that are uber advanced or just not fit for the sport, but I will try to simplify and explain the best I can because what we understand, we apply perfectly. What will follow has been tested and proved with athletes of mine and with many of my colleagues who I learned from and shared the good and not so good experiences.

Before we move on to the actual programming and workouts, we need to dig in the basics. Those notions are very important to understand so you don't miss a step and fail to get results since these laws are the main pillars of each of your programs. Once you understand these bases, the rest seems to fall into place very quickly.

The repetitions

Reps are the foundation of any program design, but as you will soon learn, reps are not just about lifting a bar a number of times, for a few sets, and call it a workout. A few seconds can decide if you go towards gaining strength or training for hypertrophy, which are two different ways of training.
The goal will determine the load.
1.1

Objective	Reps/sets	% of max
Strength/power	1-3	85-100%
Strength	3-6	75-85%
Hypertrophy	6-12 (12+)	60-75%
Endurance/metabolic	12-15+	60-%

Depending on your personal goals, your workouts would gravitate around the given reps schemes.

However, not all reps are created equal. Speed is a major factor when you strength train. When fatigue builds, the bar doesn't move as fast. Or you can do 12 repetitions in under 20 seconds. Which is why the concept of tempo is coming in.

Tempo, or time under tension, is the speed of each repetition. So if we keep the same chart as before but put in the tempo instead of reps, this is who it would look like.

1.2

Objective	T.U.T.	% of max
Strength/power	Under 10 seconds	85-100%
Strength	10-40 seconds	75-85%
Hypertrophy	40-90 seconds	60-75%
Endurance/metabolic	90+seconds	60-%

In our training programs, the tempo will be written in this matter;

4-0-1-0

4 is the eccentric portion of the movement such as the lowering of the bar to the chest on the benchpress or when you are lowering yourself on the pullups.

The first **0** is the isometric part in the stretch position, like when the bar touches the chest on the bench or when you are hanging from the pullup bar.

1 is concentric when you push or pull the bar or free weights.

The last **0** is again concentric in the fully contracted position such as when the chest touches the bar in the pullups or when the elbows are locked at the starting position in the benchpress.

So if the tempo is **4-0-1-0**, we know that each repetition is 5 seconds. So if the goal is hypertrophy, we need to do at least 8 repetitions and 3 to 4 repetitions would get the job done for strength.

Now, you have also seen in the previous charts a percentage. This detail is very important to continuously improve and get stronger. This percentage is in relation to the maximum weight you can lift if you were to do only 1 repetition on that given lift.

One of the questions I get the most from beginners is how one can set the proper weight. Since we never know (and often shouldn't even try to) what is our 1 repetition maximum weight, we often start with a "ball park" weight and go from there. I would never advise using your full 8 RM weight on the bar on the first set anyways.

If you were to do 4 sets of 8 repetitions, It would look like this;

1st set: 60% of 8 rep max
2nd set: 75% of 8 rep max
3rd set: 85% of 8 rep max
4th set: 95% of 8 rep max

As you can see, I left a little bit of energy in the tank. I rarely suggest going at 100%, unless it is the last week of the program or near the culmination of a phase, I always leave 1 or 2 reps in the tank. What happens is that that the next time around, there is always some improvement. You always end up doing more using the previous weeks' weights, which is always improvement in my book.

So the basic rule to set the proper weight is this if you can do more than 2 reps than the target rep range, increase your weight. If you can't do a clean and controlled repetition while reaching the target repetition, it is probably too heavy, especially if you are on your first set.

Supersets (agonist/antagonist)

When it comes to working out, I don't like to waste my time. I always go for the "most bang for your bucks" methods and exercises. In order to do so, the perfect principle is the agonist/antagonist pairing method. Let's say you do biceps curls. The antagonist's muscle is the triceps. The role of the triceps, in this case, would be to decelerate or just relax to not impede the work of the biceps. Another way to illustrate this would be when we pull on someone's Gi sleeve or lapel. The agonist muscles would be the back biceps, rear delt and trapezius. The antagonist muscles would be the pectorals, shoulders, rotator cuffs and even the abs would get involved. If these weren't supporting the agonist's muscles, letting go suddenly would apply such torque on your vertebras that they would probably shatter from the pulling forces. Every muscle that pushes are the agonists and the antagonists are those who are stabilizing, relaxing or decelerating the agonists.

Using this method has many advantages. In my opinion, the most important aspect of this method is that it ensures the balance between both sides, read strength qualities, like pushing and pulling, which are one of the most important aspects of grappling. However, in this case, you rarely push with both limbs at the same time, but I have the solution for that as you will see in some of the specialized exercises.

The volume

Volume is referred to as the volume of work or quantity. The volume of training is often calculated by the number of sets you do per workout. You could do 15 to 20 sets per workout (5 exercises of 3 sets) which could be considered high volume or you could do 10-12 sets (2 exercises of 5 sets) which are considered low volume.

Important rule: Volume is inversely proportional to intensity. Meaning that you can't have high volume and high intensity.

Intensity

Intensity is the percentage of your maximum weight used, as seen in the 1.2 charts of time under tension. It is not, I repeat, not something to describe how hard your workout is. Rolling is intense, especially with a higher belt. Training intensity is how close you are from maximum effort, your 1RM.

Working on strength requires a higher percentage of your 1RM than working with hypertrophy. Working with heavier weight, close to your 1RM puts a toll on your nervous system so doing endless sets can only burn you out. This is why volume and intensity are inversely proportional, they can't both be high or low at the same time.

Strength training – low volume – high intensity
hypertrophy – high volume – low intensity

What weight?

What is the correct weight to use?

This is probably one of the questions I get the most. My answer is always; I don't know! You are the one who holds the barbells and dumbells. Let's say that your goal is to do between 6 to 8 repetitions. You have to choose a weight that you obviously can handle for that amount of reps. However, you have to take into consideration that you have to do 4 sets. If you overshoot, you won't respect the rep scheme for all 4 sets right? Grab a weight you can do for 8 reps max, then at the 4th set, you should be able to stick in between 6 and 8 reps.

Also, never start with your max weight. Always leave a few reps in the tank. This is by far, one of the pieces of advice I should have stuck with. My nature is to go all out or nothing and it backfired a few years ago when I had problems with my adrenals.

You have to leave some space for constant progression. For example, let's say that you beat last week's score by 2.5 or 5 lbs already and you have a set left, GOOD!! Keep the weight and leave some for the following workout. Chances are that with proper rest and recuperation, you'll be able to lift more than if you were to go all out and couldn't increase at the next workout.

Your body has to have some room for rest. If you burn out, it takes longer to regenerate, so you might not be fully rested and ready for the next session. As long as you follow a constant progression, you will get great results.

Now you have 2 choices, you could skip and go straight to the programs or you could just keep reading and find out a few secrets. The next few paragraphs are for those who have a few years of experience in strength training or after you have done all workouts in this book, you come back to this section of the book and apply what you are about to read.

Without changing a whole lot of the workouts in this book, or your own program design, you can tweak them out a little bit and call that a new phase.

The best workout you will ever do is the workout you never did. If that is the only thing you can take from this chapter, my goal has been achieved, which is to give you basic principles that will build your foundation for a strong(er) and more performing you.

One of the first principles you will encounter in training is Adaptation, meaning the adjustment of an organism to its environment and the main feature of living species. Adaptation is the other builder and absolutely necessary if you want results. No one gets better after a workout and in fact, we become weaker. Improvement happens because the body adapts to the training load. Then comes accommodation often considered a general law of biology. Accommodation is the decrease in response of a biological object to a continued stimulus[i]. It can make you doubt, it can put you down, it will slow you down and make you comfortable if you stick to it long enough, and that's not a good thing. From accommodation, you enter the comfort zone. The thing is that this zone will sneak in and you will like it. However, only a few will manage to get out of it and push the boundaries and change for the next phase. Accommodation is when some people will make the biggest mistake in strength and conditioning, keep going without changing because it is a known terrain, they are comfortable where they are and with what they do.

If you passed the beginner stage of weight training, you know when you should change your workout programs. It is when you fail to see progress or feel strong in a workout. You seem to be doing the same thing over again and no change whatsoever on the bars, on paper or in the shape. No more adaptation, now it has become stagnation and soon procrastination.

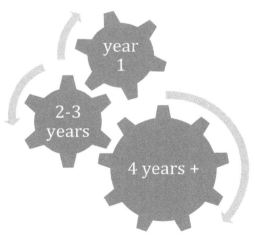

Adaptation is one of the primary principles of strength and conditioning. You see, the first year of training, the body is like a newborn, it learns and is like a sponge. This is most probably where you will gain the most results, the result of the so called adaptation principle. The trick is to keep your workouts long enough for them to keep getting results, but not too long so that you get used to it and start stalling, the dreaded plateau. In the first year, you can easily stay on the same program for a good 4 to 6-8 weeks. In the second and third years, progress doesn't come that easy, unfortunately, even when all the elements are on your side. Measure progress and measure often. The only way you can know for a fact that something is working. After 2 years, 3-4 to 6 weeks should be how often you change your programs. After 4-5 years, then experience settles in and you can figure out when and how often you change your hypertrophy/strength workouts/phases as nobody has the same ability to maintain high volume or intensity.

Beginner and advanced, we must continually challenge our muscles for growth and strength. So then, to counter adaptation, another more "important" principle is to overload the muscle. It will improve neural pathways, help muscles produce more force to handle heavier weights. It also stimulates bone growth and strengthens ligaments. Your muscles will also absorb and synthesize more protein, while preventing catabolism, gaining muscle fibers to grow larger muscles.

You absolutely need adaptation and in fact, exercise has always been an adaptive process. If you don't adapt, there is no progress. The body reacts by increasing fitness, power, strength and/or hypertrophy to go beyond the demand of the given tasks. So basically, exercise is a stress, which the body responds to by increasing its physical abilities to adapt to this given stress. Not enough stress, no adaptation occurs nor improvement. If stress is too much, injuries or overtraining may occur. Careful planning and the use of principles timed correctly will bring you results as long as you don't fall into the plateau trap for too long.

There are many tricks you can do to help you out of that freakin plateau and will force adaptation to bring you to new heights.

Increase volume

Do more sets. Let's say you usually do 3-4 sets of 8-10 reps. Keep the reps the same and do 5-6 sets of 8-10 reps. The simple increase in volume will push over your boundaries and stimulate new growth and strength.

Play with the reps
Use the same weight but manipulate the reps.

Increase the resistance
Obviously…

Play with intensity, as in more work in less time or work for a given time with less recovery.

Instead of the old boring textbook 3 sets of 8-10 reps or 4 sets of 6-8 reps, Vince Gironda used a technique called 10-8-6-15. As you increase the reps for each set, you finish up with a lighter set as what he used to explain as a pump set to drive blood into the muscle. We also know that the potentiation effect of the increasing weight of each set will also help increase your 15 RM weight aka the pump set, meaning that you can potentially take 5-8% more weight on your 15 RM that you would normally do.

Now, playing with reps and sets will take some planning and careful attention to details since you can't increase both at the same time, but not impossible unless it's planned. Here is why you should have a plan, a big picture of what you want to accomplish over a given period of time.

Most who don't abide by the periodization principle will tell you that it is impossible to plan ahead since no one can precisely predict what can happen over the course of 6 months and they are absolutely right. Nonetheless, you can always at least have a plan in general details, guidelines to follow. Most Olympic coaches and athletes have a very detailed yearly plan but it is not necessary for most of us. Here is something very basic you can use with the previously mentioned intensity and volume variations.

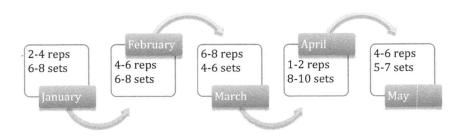

Very simple and this is only an example of how you can play around with months, weeks, sets and reps. For example, those who have a tendency to over train may have to do shorter phases on high volume and low intensity (Strength) phases.

Another way to force your body into a new adaptation is to add energy system workouts, which are great to include in a yearly plan.

With the growing belief that cardio/energy system work will burn muscle, where many popular Fitness personalities claim that doing more than 20 minutes of cardio will make you lose hard-earned muscle mass, it makes it easy to be scared of anything that will bring your heart rate up for long periods of time. Big guys be like I'm not bringing the groceries up a flight of stairs in fear of losing my pump in the upper pecs from Monday's chest workout. What they can't seem to get is the fact that it is way, way more complicated than that. In fact, cardiovascular training can help your gains in many ways.

Myths and old ways for cardiovascular training are often thrown around by physique competitors, with the notion that in order to lose fat, you abso'frekin'lutely need to do 30 minutes of cardio with an empty stomach in the morning to be on your way to contest shape. Well, there are many roads that lead to Rome.

Enter interval training or more commonly known as HIIT – High intensity interval training. I will save you the details since there are so many great articles on the subjects. All you need to know is that you need to work for a given time followed by rest periods and do a given number of sets. Doesn't it sound like weight lifting? Interval training has been proven to be more effective in burning fat and improving cardiovascular capacities.

We have been thought for many years that the exercise specificity is primordial and should be as close as possible to the outcome (specific exercise task or performance criteria). A study[ii] from burgomaster et al. (2007) makes us rethink the long-held belief of training adaptation and specificity and also, a reminder that for some people, intense training will be more time-efficient and have the same effect and as potent as the submaximal endurance type workouts. This study reported that 6 weeks of low-volume, high-intensity sprint training-induced similar changes in selected whole-body and skeletal muscle adaptations as traditional high-volume, low-intensity endurance workouts undertaken for the same intervention period.

Specifically, they revealed that 4-6x 30 sec sprints separated by 4–5 min of passive recovery 3 days/week resulted in comparable increases in markers of skeletal muscle carbohydrate metabolism, lipid oxidation, and mitochondrial biogenesis as when subjects undertook 40–60 min of continuous submaximal cycling a day for 5 days/week. Particularly impressive given that weekly training volume was ~90% lower in the sprint-trained group resulting in total cumulative training time of ~1.5 compared to 4.5 h per week.

So circuit training and HIIT are the best choices to get the most benefits in less time. Studies have also stated a diminution in total cholesterol levels while levels of HDL-cholesterol, increased with circuit style training. Through regular circuit training routines, individuals can increase their oxygen utilization capabilities. Capillaries supply blood and oxygen and remove waste, as these actions are obviously necessary. Due to the demands placed on different parts of your body during exercise, the ability of your capillaries to respond to your body's needs plays an important role in fatigue and endurance and this is why you should also include in your workouts some type of cardiovascular training throughout the year.

While there is plenty of research that proves cardiovascular training has benefits, people tend to forget that there are not only the treadmill or mile long runs to help increase your cardio capabilities. My personal favorite is the modified strongman type training. In any workout, the goal is to put the first few exercises with the most bangs for your buck effect, meaning that you need big compound exercises. So for strongman training, grab 2-3 exercises and alternate them in supersets for a given amount of time. Let's have a 1 to 1 ratio, meaning you rest as much as you work. So for a working time of 3 minutes, you rest 3 minutes.

A1 Barbell deadlift x5

A2 Prowler push for 120 feet

A3 Standing log press x 5

Stop when needed but as little as possible. The goal is to repeat the circuit as many times as possible in 3 minutes. Do 5 sets and call it a day.

Let's get back to muscle pumpin' sleeve bustin' lift things up and put them down principles.

Another way I use to declare war on muscle is the 'Dual Method" principle…I combine two principles into one workout. For example:

Mechanical advantage + drop sets

A1 Frenchpress high pulley x12, no rest

A2 Rope pushdown x8-10 + 2 x drop set -5% each, rest 60 seconds

A3 Preacher curl x 12, no rest

A4 standing curl x8-10 +2x drop sets-5% each, rest 120 seconds

You may have to drop 8-10% of the weight off at every set. You begin Triceps and Biceps with isolation exercises to bring the most out of them from the get-go followed by the easiest exercises since technique will be the first thing to go, especially with the drop sets. So for the Mechanical advantage principle, start with the toughest and finish with the easiest technically speaking.

I'm sure you are thinking many other strategies you would love to try or that might have been in your training bucket list for a while. My best advice would be to do it NOW! Don't wait, it will most probably throw you into new growth or on a new path.

Don't wait until adaptation becomes accommodation and enjoy your workouts!

Training Frequency

I think that training frequency is the most confusing issue for anyone trying to include weight lifting to their training/rolling plan. In fact, it is a very personal concept to approach. No one is the same. Some may be able to deal with a high volume of training when others will have a hard time to adapt to short, twice a week workouts.

Although most can manage a few weeks of intense workouts, the goal is to be able to recover from them. This is why the periodization principle is so important. It helps you recover from specialized phases. Strength training phases demand more emphasis on recovery, especially when combined with BJJ, due to the elevated risks of injuries.

The question is, how many strength/weight lifting workouts can we do in a week to be realistic?

The more rolling sessions you get in, the better you will become, and faster. AS true as it is, you have to find your own training frequency. Some have reported better technique retention when training 4 times a week, others absolutely need to get 5 or 6 classes out of 7 days. The thing is that you can easily manage the workload. 2 days of drilling only with another 2 days of rolling plus techniques can be very valuable. The other 2 days could be given to strength training and one day of complete recovery.

Depending on how many weight training sessions you want to fit in a week, and how you can manage to make sure that nutrition can stay up to par due to increased caloric expenditure, you might have to re-think the days and time you practice, train and eat. It goes without saying that they are all interdependent with each other. It will be a constant battle for equilibrium between the three. If your goal is to gain muscle, you'll need to lift weights more and improve recovery, where you will have to cut down on Jits rolling for a while to maximize recovery. If you want to improve some technical aspects, you'll have to invest more on time on the mats and drilling and have a minimum of weight lifting, for injury prevention as an example.

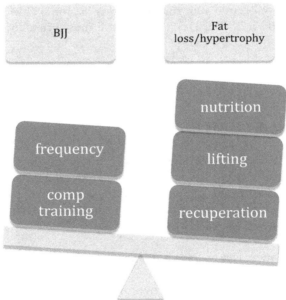

Now let's get down to business.

Depending on your goals and objectives, you can start wherever you want in the roll strong(er) workouts, but I would highly suggest that you start from scratch, with the rehab/prehab first. What it will do is it will probably fix a few issues and pains. If you went through the first evaluation in chapter 2, evaluated your needs and succeeded with flying colors, then skip it as you wish and go right to the hypertrophy or strength sections.

Before we start, It would be highly irresponsible of me to let you start without caution, and start any of my exercise programs. I always lead my clients towards having a full health rundown from their family doctors before starting any physical activity and/or diet. This might be the most important advice in the book. You never know what could show up in blood test and starting a diet or an exercise plan without knowing your full health profile, where we can find underlying health issues like diabetes, heart conditions, or any health concern can only make it worst.

No program is perfect and the perfect program does not exist. I designed these with one intention in mind. Constant progression. The following is for those who have done a very low score on all the tests outlined in evaluating your needs section.

	Exercise	Sets	Reps	Tempo	Rest
A	DB step up	3	20	1010	60
B	Flat db press close grip	3	15	2020	60
C	Hip extension	3	15	2010	60
D	Reverse grip lat-pulldown	3	12-15	3010	60
E	Side bridge	3	10	3010	60

All exercises are to be done for 3 sets. Once the given sets are done for a given exercise then on to the next one. It can be done 2 to 3 times a week. Usually, beginners can keep this format for a while, for about 6 to 8 weeks.

The more experience you gain, the faster you will change your programs. Beginners can experience significant strength gains. They can gain as much as 25% or more in the first three to six months, note Jack H. Wilmore and David L. Costill, authors of "Physiology of Sport and Exercise" After more than one year of experience, the general rule is to change programs every 4 weeks or after having repeated them between 4 to 6 times keep seeing progress.

The second phase could look like this one.

Day1 Upper body

	Exercise	Sets	Reps	Tempo	Rest
A1	Benchpress	3	10-12	3010	60

A2	Lat-pulldown	3	10-12	3010	60
B1	Seated external rotation	3	10-12	3010	60
B2	Seated row (neutral grip)	3	10-12	3010	60
C1	Triceps lying extension BB	3	12-15	3010	60
C2	Low pulley ez bar curls	3	12-15	3010	60
D	Neck extension Iso on ball	3	6-8	1310	60

Day 2

	Exercise	Sets	Reps	Tempo	Rest
A1	DB step up	3	20-25	1010	60
A2	Unilateral swiss ball hip extension & curl	3	12-15	2222	60
B1	Leg press	3	12-15	3010	60
B2	Lying leg curl	3	8-10	3010	60
C1	Seated calf raise	3	15-20	3010	60
C2	QL lift (side plank)	3	8-10	1310	60

By dividing the program into two parts, there is more work done per body part. The key to gaining muscle mass is more workout volume, as in more sets and reps. A study whose results were published in "The Journal of Applied Physiology" shows that high volume is the most important factor for gaining muscle mass.

Recently meta-analysis published in "The Journal of Strength and Conditioning Research" reveals that multiple-series workouts have resulted in 46% strength gains and 40% increase in muscle growth compared to several protocols.

Now that you have established a good base, we are ready to move on to the specialized training design for Brazilian Jujitsu. But before we dig into the details, due to the fact that some of you won't have access to some machines and/or given exercises, I am about to give you a little rundown of the how/what/when you can choose certain exercise over others in hope of teaching you a thing or two about how to manipulate your workouts with the resources you might have and to the level you are at to improve some of the most important aspects of your game.

How to choose exercises.

Choosing the exercises according to your experience is a basic concept that will allow you to choose according to your needs and your experience. Generally, at the beginning the coordination is weak and it is perfectly normal. So the recommendation is to use mostly machines always including some exercises with free dumbbells. With experience and more coordination, the majority of your training will be done with dumbbells and free bars. Once experience, coordination, strength, and endurance are acquired, you can vary your workouts with Olympic lifts that are described as complex exercises.

The following is a modification of Dietmar Schmidtbleicher's organizational chart regarding activation levels. Sweden's Riccard Nillson and Charles Poliquin added the seventh level.

Compound Against Isolated Exercises (Neuromuscular activity - NMA) Dietmar Schmidtbleicher, (Ricard Nillson, Charles Poliquin added level 7)

1- Isolation exercise with a variable resistance machine. (ie Leg extension on cam machine type i.e. Cybex Leg Extension, DAVID Leg curl)

2- Complex exercise with a variable resistance machine. (ie Leg press on machine Nautilus, LifeFitness Incline Press Machine)

3- Insulation exercise with constant resistance machine. (ie Scott pulley curls, Triceps pressdown on pulley machine.)

4- Complex exercise with machine with constant resistance. (ie Leg press on standard machine)

5- Insulation exercise with free dumbbells. (ie Scott barbell curls, lying flyes)

6- Complex exercise with free dumbbells. (ie Snatch pulls, power cleans)

7- Complex Exercise with Free Dumbbells (ie Power Snatch, dips on rings, rope climbing)

The majority of people start with level 4 exercises. Despite the fact that all these little exercises are fairly simple, there are countless youtube channels that have practically all the exercises in the bank by coaches of all levels. However, nothing beats a good coach, in person, that can help you climb the ladder faster and safer.

Grip strength.

The missing link in almost every training program is grip strength. If your grip can't hold the loads during a workout, it will probably give out in intense rolls, especially in competitions. Exercises such as deadlift, chin-ups or squats with HEX bar are the exercises that will give you big results, but if your grip can't follow, you'll see your results stagnate. Some equipment that can help you a lot are thick barbells or small additions like FatGripz or GripsFear that can be carried with you and can be installed on any type of bar.

Here is a small forearm program that you'll feel deep down to your bones.

	Exercise	Sets	Reps	Tempo	Rest
A1	Elbow flexion pronated grip wide grip	4	8	2020	0
A2	Elbow flexion pronated grip medium grip	4	8	2020	0
A3	Elbow flexion neutral grip	4	Max out (15-20)	2020	90
B1	Standing Wrist flexion bar behind back	3	12	2010	0
B2	Wrist extension forearms on flat bench	3	12	2010	60
C	Wrist flexion, forearms on bench with DB	3	Max out (15-20)	2020	60

It turns out that your grip strength could be used as a predictor test for longevity. It can be highly predictive of functional limitations and years of disability. "Physicians or other health care professionals can measure grip strength to identify patients with serious conditions such as heart failure or other heart conditions who have a particularly high risk of dying from their disease," says Dr. Darryl Leong, Researcher and Assistant Professor of Medicine at McMaster University Michael G. of Medicine and Cardiology.

Based on their studyxix of 140,000 adults aged between 35-70 years and followed over a 4-year period in 17 countries, the results revealed that for every 5 kilograms (11 pounds) drop in grip strength, one in six had an increased risk of death from any cause[6].

The gripping force was a strong predictor of cardiovascular disease mortality for people from a variety of economic and socio-cultural backgrounds. These results suggest that muscle strength is a risk factor for cardiovascular disease and can even predict the risk of death in people who develop cardiovascular or non-cardiovascular disease. These findings will help researchers design a way to improve muscle strength in patients and increase their life expectancy.

The core and low back are also sources of concern. Most complaints of beginners are about the low back and ribs that take a beating. The first few rolls are always mind-blowingly deadly since all you try to do is survive and you don't obviously know what you have to do to get out of a mounted position for example. All you learn is to bridge and roll, or bridge to break the opponent's posture and try to bring your knees to regard.

Breaking down the bridge and the shrimping involved in some of the drills, the low back, and hip flexors are put to the test. However, to bridge and shrimp under pressure often becomes twisting of the spine with your opponent as a resistance, a full 100lbs+ or more. It is not something you can replicate with an exercise, and in fact, you shouldn't. However, this article is not about how to perfect the technique, but how to prevent injuries. To perfect the technique, put more time on the mat.

To protect the spine and the core, besides better technique, core muscles need to be in somewhat of a great condition. Meaning that they have to be structurally functional. To understand functional strength, you need also to start thinking further than just your abs, because core strength starts from the extremities; it's not just about sporting a set of great abs and

---

[6] A similar study is linked to other aging markers, such as mortality, disability, cognitive decline, and the ability to recover from subjects hospital stays. The researchers analyzed more than 50 studies of people from all over the world and of all ages and found that a 65-year-old white woman with no high school education had the same grip strength as a 69-year-old white woman had completed high school. This suggests that less educated people with less access to health care may have lower grip strength, which is associated with lower life expectancy, higher rates of illness, and faster cognitive decline.

call it a day.

What is harder to perform, a leg raise or a knee raise? Is a sit up harder with your arms up over your head or with your arms on your side?

Core begins with the extremities. The further you hold a weight in front of you, the harder your core will try to stabilize. If you were to hold the weight in front of you, your lower back would fire up and your abs would be the antagonist helping out. If you were to hold a weight in the back of you, your abs would fire up to hold you straight and your low back would be the antagonist helping out by stabilizing and making sure you stay upright.

In jits, drilling the techniques makes you use less strength and more flow while being effective at performing the given technique without using too much strength, preserving energy. However, in the meantime, you'll make mistakes, which often lead to injuries. When it comes to core muscles, you don't just rely on abs or lower back, there is also deep muscle tissue such as the Quadratus lumborum, the transverse abdominous, hip flexors, psoas, internal and external obliques. Although in the back, the erector spine and multifidus play a big role in the core as well. Even the fascia, the sheet of connective tissue, primarily collagen, beneath the skin that attaches, stabilizes, encloses, and separates muscles and other internal organs, go up to the neck and down to the toes. So basically, they all have one goal in common, to protect the spine at all costs.

As soon as forces are being applied on the limbs, the core muscles contract to counter the weight and stabilize the trunk. So in general, thinking of core should define a movement as a whole and a chain of muscles working together to counter the applied force.

Core muscles are best developed with exercises like deadlifts, pullups, presses and all types of squats and benchpress. Sure, there is always the crunches, sit-ups and leg raises, which are the basics and in almost any body's weight lifting plan, but like I mentioned earlier, core also comes from the extremities and is complex recruitment from the nervous system (in this case) of the fight to survive situation. You will need one or both arms and legs to support or hold an opponent while the other limbs try to grab or block something to gain advantage, in just a few seconds. Which is why multi-joint or compound exercises do a better job. They involve more than one joint or muscle group at a time.

Then there is the neck. One of the first things we learn in martial arts, in general, is that the head controls the rest of the body. Move the head and the body follows. So it goes without saying that a strong neck can save you from a few bad situations. After a few months of guillotine and choke drills, you'll notice a few gains in the traps generally. The major pains in the neck (literally) are the mid-back (trapezius 2-3) and scalene muscles, which are often twisted and stretched to their limits while rolling and trying to resist those chokes. Unfortunately, it's part of the game.

For neck training purposes, I would advise to go with very light loads. These are very small muscles and are easily strainable.

My go-to exercise to train the neck extensors is the swiss ball neck support.

Level 1 which is done upright while you are holding the ball with the back of your head against the wall. Use a 3 second isometric contraction (push your head in the ball at max 25% effort) for about 3 sets of 10 reps.

Level 2 is done by bridging with only your head and shoulders on the ball, as the starting position. The goal is to lift your shoulders off the ball while pushing your head into the ball for 3 sets of 5 repetitions of 5 seconds isometric contractions.

Strength curves

Each exercise and machine has its own strength curves, depending on the position of the body, your strength and/or experience, you can manipulate to your advantage or disadvantage. Mainly, an exercise that becomes easier towards the end of the concentric amplitude (elbow extension or when your arm is almost straight) has an upward curve as with the benchpress. The pull up can also be taken as an example when the movement becomes more and more difficult with amplitude (elbow flexion or when the arm is fully bent) so it's a downward curve. A so-called concave (bell) curve becomes more difficult in the middle of the amplitude as flexion of the elbow. A quick way to change the strength curves is to only change the angles of the body.

My favorite way to change the strength curve of an exercise is to use chains or elastic bands. The chains increase the resistance gradually, one link at a time. They increase the mechanical advantage by reducing the load to the most difficult position and increasing it to the easiest position. This method helps the development of strength, and also indirectly work the stabilizers because the chains create a slight instability during the lifts.

Depending on the size of the chain, each link can weigh between .50 and 1 lb. Let's say you have 100 pounds of weight on the bar. At the starting position (straight arms), you will have 130 lbs on the bar (100 lbs + 15 lbs of chains on each side). During the descent, you will remove 2 lbs from each link that touches the floor. Once you reach the chest, you will have 115 lbs. During the concentric push, you will add 15 lbs of chain, 2 lbs to each link that will take off from the floor and return to 130 lbs at the beginning of the movement. This tool is very useful for developing strength.

The elastic bands, however, add an exponential resistance. However, I must warn you that rubber bands are extremely difficult, must be used intelligently and are reserved for experienced trainees. They increase the speed of the bar in eccentric, which requires the athlete to apply even more resistance during the descent. Let's keep our benchpress example. Unfortunately, with several varieties of benchpress, the possibility of adding elastic bands is still quite rare. You can find this type of benchpress in specialized gyms (read hardcore). You can also use the squat cages so that the elastic bands are attached to the bars and at the bottom of the cage.

With elastics, the bar will weigh only 45 lbs. In the chest, but you will have almost 3 times the weight of full flexion. Use elastics for speed. With controlled movement and good technique, mix fast and slow repetitions. With a good spotter, do about 8 repetitions until concentric failure or until you are no longer able to do another repetition and have to remove the bar. Your spotter must remove the elastics during the 10 seconds of rest allocated. You then take the bar and continue the series, again, until you are no longer able to do another. The feeling is unbearable, but the results will be incredible.

Angles

The benches are often always at the same angles, 45 °, 30 °, flat or declined at 15-20 °. So, without ever really changing your workout or exercise, from one workout to another, you can change the angles by about 10 °, so the angle of attack will always be varied while keeping the same charge and adding a little more difficulties.

CHAPTER 7

ENERGY SYSTEMS

There is a great deal of importance surrounding cardiovascular work. Of the many benefits that cardiovascular work provides, improving work capacity is the one that we are seeking the most. It also improves heart health, increases your resting metabolic rate, meaning that you become a fat-burning machine, even at rest. But one of the major benefits, in my opinion, is that it helps to reduce your DOMS (delayed onset of muscle soreness) and help the muscle tissue in the repair and rebuilding process. To you, it means that you will roll easier, faster and recuperate much faster.

According to the Journal of Applied Physiology, Nutrition, and Metabolism, researchers concluded that high-intensity interval training (HIIT) is a very powerful method to increase whole-body skeletal muscle capacities to oxidize fat and carbohydrates in previously untrained individuals. However, the fact that it was done on untrained individuals might have boosted the results. So if they have some kind of results, most people will. But due to one basic law, the principle of adaptation, your results will stagnate eventually.

You need to build endurance at first and that is why most can't take the first roll. The same goes for those who are sidelined after a while, the first few fights, even though they have more experience, are like getting hit by a train right in the chest.

Staying calm and composed while rolling takes getting used too. You will get in compromising situations and you will panic. That's when you will use too much strength, you will breed (or not) a lot faster, and that is also when lactic acid builds up. This build-up let's muscle fatigue creep in and that is when you can't take it and burn out.

Learning how to breed and focus your energy when you need is a really big deal. Besides the fact that you will learn most of it as you gain more experience, there are a few tips and tricks on how you can manage lactic acid and improve your cardiovascular capabilities.

First things first, when you start your journey in BJJ, you quickly get the wake-up call that even though you thought you were in shape or in somewhat of a good conditioning base, you obviously weren't.

Training the energy systems is essential if you want to improve your game. There is obviously no better to improve your cardio then by rolling and practicing what you have just learned and drilling it non stop. However, as you will become better and understand more of the concepts, you'll become much better at preserving energy while rolling. So no great improvement, probably just maintenance. Then again, to push boundaries, you'll have to roll harder, but it doesn't actually translate to good rolls.

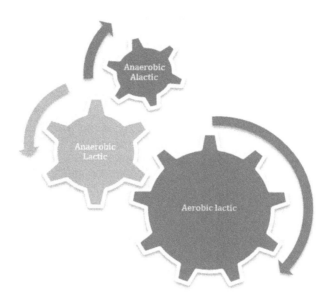

There are three main folders in which you can categorize your energy systems.
jus

Anaerobic Alactic (AA) has lots of power output but lasts only for about 15 to 20 seconds

Anaerobic Lactic (AAL) is a perfect mix of power and endurance and can last as much as 2 minutes.

Aerobic Lactic (AL)is the endurance brother of them all and kicks in long bouts that go beyond 2 minutes.

Looking at the previous anagrams, once the Anaerobic Alactic system starts, all the systems are ready to kick in, it all depends on how long the effort is. The first wheel will spin very fast but has the power to move all three wheels but can't last long so once the power has drained out, after a few seconds, the Anaerobic lactic system kicks in and once this system is out of juice, after about 90 to 120 seconds, the aerobic system kicks in and could last for hours if trained well. The difference is that the aerobic system has a very small power output compared to the AA.

Looking at this, AA would be when you try to fight your way out of crossed or working for a takedown, AL would be the end of a 5 to 8 minute round and AAL would be drilling. As you can see You spend a lot of time in between, but you don't want to use too much strength as you'll gas out fast and you can't roll for too long as you'll burn yourself out.

You can improve all of them but you will never have them all. The goal is to be able to use them wisely. To train them, I suggest to use phases that we will explore in detail in the periodization chapter. Working on all strength qualities at once is counterproductive in many ways since endurance and cardio works impair strength gains. Working on gaining lean muscle mass can't be done with extensive cardio sessions as well since all gains are slowed down with lots of cardiovascular work as well. We will look at different models of periodization you'll be able to use throughout the year to help you plan your game around competitions and this will improve your game tremendously.

First things first, let's say that you are just starting training and need more cardiovascular work to improve your rolling or sparring sessions.

Most studies on interval training agree that this type of training improves insulin sensitivity, cardiorespiratory fitness, and the mitochondrial content of skeletal muscle.

Due to the high-intensity demands of this type of training, a good base is required. If you never stepped into a gym before or did any type of cardiovascular work, starting with this type of training can and will kill you (it happened a few times literally since some start all out without any health checks or previous consultations). The best way to do this, and the only true time that it is useful, is by doing slow and steady pace cardiovascular training. Meaning that you have to build up your endurance first by doing 20-30 minutes of steady pace cardio, like on a treadmill or bike. You keep your heart rate at about 60-70% of your maximum heart rate.

You remember when, or if you are a white belt, the first few rolls? Having a hard time breathing, gasping after only 1 or 2 minutes of a "light roll"? Well this is exactly it. Rolling is a type of interval training but only when you know how to roll. You start slow, attack gradually, try, to land your first takedown and once you land it, you establish base, stabilize, and move on. In other words, short bursts of intense work followed by short rest. The best way to apply it in BJJ is obviously and will always be roll sessions. No one can deny that. In spite of this, you can better your game by working once or twice a week of the mat or when injury keeps you off the mats.

Once you have done 4 to 6 weeks of slow and steady cardiovascular endurance, you can now start by incorporating some interval work in your schedule and let go of endurance work. Endurance capacity is maintained as long as you keep working on aerobic work and capacity[7].

Here's a simple way to go for the next 12 weeks with 2-3 workouts per week with the device of your choice. It is recommended to do it after your weight lifting sessions.

HIIT Cardio beginner workout

Week	High intensity	Low intensity	sets
1	15sec	2min 45sec	4
2	15	2:30	4
3	30	2:30	5
4	30	2:15	5
5	45	2:15	5
6	----	30 min	1
7	45sec	120 sec	6
8	60	120	6
9	60	105	7
10	60	90	7
11	90	90	6
12	60	60	8

High intensity/work requires max effort, meaning that you push as hard as you can for the given time (ex: 30 seconds).

---

[7] If you stop everything, don't think that you'll keep your endurance! Some people think that you gain it all back as soon as you start again which is never the case, for any strength or cardio capacity. You need to slowly get back up after long set backs. The shorter the set back, the fastest it will come back.

Next phase for interval training would be to go with the needs of our sport. We want to increase our work capacity and by doing so, we can recuperate faster[8]. Rolling for simple classes or for competition are two different, many different things. In this case, you can fight for 5 minutes straight, with periods of lower and higher intensity. Hockey players will have shifts of 45 to 60 seconds at a time. You can be a linebacker and push as hard as possible for 10-15 seconds against what can possibly be an immovable force.

Once the needs are identified, you can get as close as possible to it and build a few conditioning sessions a week to keep improving your cardiovascular capacity.

Being able to maintain your Heart rate at 80%+ of your max for extended periods of time needs preparation. Being able to do so will help you manage to fight at higher intensity and in return help you make better decisions under this kind of pressure.

HIIT complete workout

For these types of sessions, you might have to push yourself to the brink of death. You will have to calculate your max heart rate and quantify your sessions and results.

First, calculate your maximum heart rate with this formula:

220-age = max freq

ex:

20 years = 200 bpm

40 years = 180 bpm

N.B.: This calculation gives a general idea but varies enormously from one individual to another.

Here is how your training will take place. The goal will be to reach your maximum beats per minute in the given intervals. The timer starts as soon as you reach the target heart rate.

---

[8] The better your cardio conditioning is, the better your recovery will be.

Training twice a week HIIT. (Use the Polar Heart Rate monitor with the polar beat app)

Week 1

Warmup 3 sets of 60 seconds at 50% of the max with a rest of two minutes between each interval.

Warmup 3 sets of 60sec. at 60% max, rest 2 min between sets

Training = 5 sets of 60 sec. at 75% max. As soon as your HR goes down to 60%, you go at it again (reminder: timer starts when you reach 75% and stay there for 60sec.)

Week 2

Warmup 3 sets of 60 seconds at 55% of the max with a rest of two minutes between each interval.

Warmup 3 sets of 60sec. at 65% max, rest 2 min between sets

Training = 5 sets of 60 sec. at 80% max. Rest until 65%.

Week 3

Warmup 3 sets of 60 seconds at 65% of the max with a two-minute rest between each interval.

Warmup 3 sets of 60sec. at 75% max, rest 2 min between sets

Training = 5 sets of 45 sec. at 85% max. rest until 75%

Week 4

Warmup 3 sets of 60 seconds at 60% of the max with a two-minute rest between each interval.

Warmup 3 sets of 60sec. at 75% max, rest 2 min between sets

Training = 6 sets of 30 sec. at 90% max. First 4 sets, rest until 75%, last two sets, 80-83%.

In this case, we never allow the heart rate to go lower than 60-70% of max heart rate. Like I said previously, we try to replicate as close as possible the requirements of the given sport. When you look at a BJJ round, you never fully rest. You spend time between partial recovery (if you are lucky) and working to gain a position for submission. So alternating between periods of lower and higher intensity is what should be done outside the mats to improve work capacity. Being able to endure longer periods of higher intensity is the goal.

As you get better, you can't just sit on it. Your HR won't go as high since the game is to rely on technique over strength until you roll with someone bigger or stronger than you. Like I always say, technique over strength, until you fight someone of equal abilities, strength will save your ass.

Now, what type of equipment should you use?

I tried them all, prowler, stair masters, etc., but two made the cut. The best pieces of equipment to use in my opinion are the assault bike and the Concept 2 rower. First, being able to use the upper body is key, so the assault bike does it perfectly, but in my opinion, the rower is best. The majority of BJJ rounds are done on the floor, involving the posterior chain, arms and grip strength, which is what the rower uses best. If you go really hard at it, you can go from I'm good to destination fucked in a matter of a few seconds.

Here is one example of a training session done with the prowler. The goal was to do 30 minutes of prowler non-stop with bodyweight on the prowler. Push 60 feet high handles, push 60 feet with low handles. Rest was at every 60 feet until my HR came back down to 70% of my max. You can easily see the difference between pushing low handles vs. high handles. Low handles are harder since the body is almost horizontal, pushing the heart rate higher and faster than when the body is almost at vertical.

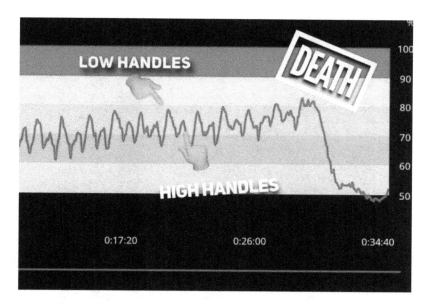

Next is a rolling session we did with about 45 minutes of drills at the beginning followed by rolls for a total of 2 hours and 20 minutes of training.

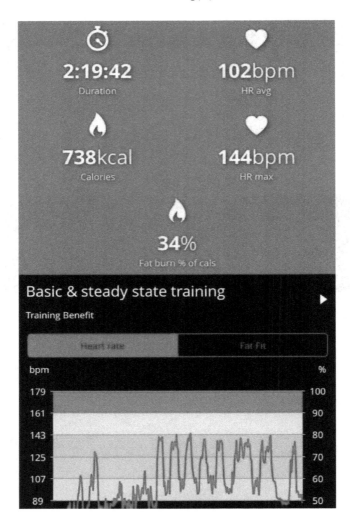

You don't absolutely have to jump on a treadmill, bike or do sprints outside to get a decent interval workout. It could be done easily by lifting weights in a circuit type matter. I do the strongman workouts to improve overall strength as much as cardiovascular capacities. What I love about these specialized workouts is that it brings back the concept of lifting and carrying heavy things. It really challenges the body to new heights.

It has to be awkward and heavy. That's how it should feel. Heavy is relative to the person that lifts things up and puts them down. It goes without saying that what is heavy for you might be light for someone else, so my advice for any type of strongman workout is to ramp up the weights gradually. This is especially true in a circuit style workout since it can bite you in the rear end sooner than you might think.

Mental toughness. I call it necessary roughness. Many get so caught up with their lifting "favorites" that they forget the adaptation principle. Gym rats will always use exercises that they master well and make them feel strong, however, as soon as they try something new they put their "tails" between their legs and find all the excuses why they sucked at it. Leave your pride at home, leave it to those big lifts and reap the rewards of real functional strength.

Let's have a look at some of the traditional strongman exercises that I use for BJJ.

Tire flips

This can be tricky since you have to find tires. But most of the tire retailers are stuck with recycling old tires and they have to pay to recycle them. So the majority of them will be glad to give you one free of charge, and they might even deliver. Having one for yourself in your backyard is great. Just be ready to get a few weird looks from your neighbors. The weights vary greatly, but it is possible to find the stats of the tires online.

Technique
The tire flip provides a high degree of physiological stress. You can split it into 4 phases.

First pull – Deadlifting from the floor, up to the hips.
Second, pull – From lower hips to lower chest with the back leg following through with a lunge.
Transition – flipping the hands from supinated to pronated.
Push off – push to flip over the tire.

The most common mistakes are having your feet too close on the first pull, which puts tremendous stress on the lower back. Having your feet under your hips and your chest against the tire (about 45' angle push-off) will save your back and provide you the best leverage.

Another mistake is in the transition phase. On the second pull, you perform a forward lunge which helps you bring up the tire a few inches, enough to flip from supinated to pronated grip.

The farmer's walk

The farmer's walk is great for general strength and conditioning. It shines for overall stamina and is also a great glute exercise. It is best done with the actual farmer's walk handles since grabbing dumbbells will result in bruised hips. Grab the handles, choose a distance and go for it. You can have a figure-eight circuit or every 3 steps, stop and go again which makes it even tougher for the grip, forearm, and upper body. It pays huge dividends on grip strength.

The most common mistake is grabbing the handle on the edges instead of the middle. This makes the weight shift forward or backward and makes you lose the grip faster.

The log

The availability of this one is limited unfortunately to gyms that invest in these particular pieces of strongman equipment. However, as with all overhead presses variations, it is an excellent all-around upper body strength developer. The added bonus is that instead of having the bar rest on the front of the shoulders which biomechanically, is where the tension is lessened. With the log, the thickness of the implement makes this position a lot harder on the spine. And believe it or not, the abs since you need to stabilize the whole upper torso. So, your upper body is tilted backward which stretches the abs and activates the lower back. Anyone who has done a great deal of training on the log can attest to that. Due to the heavy loads on the spine and upper body position, I would consider this exercise as advanced thus it requires caution.

Sleds and prowlers

These are probably the best and most versatile exercises. They allow lateral work (and do this way better than any speed ladders), heavy pushes, belted, plus they are effective for speed, rehab, sport-specific, etc. There are no real critical or faulty techniques to consider. So the amount of work and intensity you put in will be directly correlated with your results.

I love to use strongman equipment for finishers. Sometimes, when pressed for time and the inability to come more often than desired to the gym, we include strongman finishers. 10 to 15 minutes of metabolic work to finish off a workout helps the fat loss progress and for BJJ, I use it for cardiovascular training and grip strength maintenance. Here are a few tips to maximize those small but deadly sessions.

1. Even though the goal is fat loss, heavy sets with low reps and shorter rest intervals will do the job. As long as the technique is somewhat safe, go for it. The technique will always be "less than perfect" with unconventional lifts but still aim for quality over quantity, especially under fatigue.

2. Stick with prowlers, sleds, sandbags and anything not too taxing for the nervous system such as the big lifts like heavy tires, stones, and yokes. Keep in mind that you just worked out, so your nervous system is not as fresh.

3. If you still choose to do it, use the heaviest and more complex lift at the beginning, such as tire flips or logs. You could do it at the end, which inevitably makes it tougher, but you are looking for problems. The goal is fat burn, not a new hole in the log or a herniated disk.

4. You can drop in some type of Olympic lifts and bodyweight exercises for added pleasure and increased time of work.

5. Training the energy systems is best if done on a day devoted to them or on leg day.

6. You can go for sets. Example:
A1- Log press x 6, no rest
A2- Heavy sandbag over the shoulder toss x 6, rest 120 seconds, 4-5 sets.

7. Go for time. Ex: A1 A2 A3, as many sets as possible in 10 minutes.

8. Go for war. Ex: Finish as fast as possible, Ex.: prowler for distance (1000 feet), 100 deadlifts with 50% bodyweight.

9. Limited rest method. Every week, keep the same finisher but cut 20 seconds on the rest periods.

10. Upper/Lower for time method. Pick one exercise that targets the upper body and one for lower, go at it for 20 minutes. Ex.: Standing log presses and prowler, (sub max Ex.: +-70%), rest 45 seconds between or rest as needed for 20 minutes.

Now, you might not have access to these types of equipment. No worries, what follows is a few alternatives you can do without or practically no equipment or just simple things.

You own a car, perfect. Pick a distance in your street or preferably early morning or late evenings in the shopping mall parking lot. Do simple intervals as in 60 seconds of work and rest between 60 seconds to 2 minutes, depending on your current conditioning. While the simple 1 to 2, work to rest ratio is the usual starting point, you need to consider the needs of the sport.

When you start, the first 60 seconds of rolls are just unbearable. Yes, it is mostly due to a lack of conditioning, conditioning for this sport more specifically. I've seen guys in very good shape tap out in under 60 seconds of the first rolls they ever did. Why? It's totally different from anything you do cardio wise in the gym world. You can do all the cardio you want, but if you can't manage your energy efficiency while you roll, the lesson will be very hard hitting. As we say, you will have to feel like you are drowning before you really want to learn how to swim.

That is the reason why everyone, in shape or not, feels like they are drowning or major difficulty to breath in the beginning. They use too much strength and not enough technique (which they obviously don't have at the beginning) and gas out very fast. Lactic acid builds up by the lack of oxygen from improper breathing, fighting to survive hard-hitting and trying to apply the theory you just learned while your brain is going at a hundred miles per hour. Is there anything you can do that would replicate that kind of stress on the body? Not at all, except fighting and rolling.

So how the hell can you do better? What you do in the gym can also be called acquiring abilities. Your job is to take these abilities and transport them into the sport that you practice. Bobsledders can squat and deadlift huge amounts of weight but what they do is push a sled for less than 10 seconds. Are they pushing sleds relentlessly to get stronger? They get stronger in the gym and apply this new-found strength on push off which is starting strength, the required quality for their event.

Looking at it this way, we must understand that our ability to withstand this kind of cardiovascular work in short periods of time has to be mimicked in the gym to gain somewhat of better conditioning and be ready to withstand this amount of stress in short amount of time. The goal is to bring your cardio to be able to last a good 5 minutes at least, of intense work.

What we want to improve is the ability to perform for 5 minutes which is the usual time for low level belts and can go up to more than 10 minutes at higher levels, especially for those looking at the competition. Even when you have gained experience and know-how to roll efficiently, the goal is to do controlled bursts of attacks that are often followed by transitions and stalls which obviously helps to regain somewhat of a lowered heart rate and gain strategic advantages.

My favorite piece of cardio machine that I find beat the living hell out of you and you feel like you can breath at the same time is the Concept 2 rower. At the beginning of the book, you have found a way to evaluate your current state. So this is your baseline, your starting state. So if you have done the 2K in under 10 minutes, or just couldn't finish it, don't beat yourself up about it, you will get better very fast. You just have to stick with the program and commit to it.

You can use the HIIT cardio beginner workout to get you started if you never tried High-intensity interval training beforehand as it is very demanding. If you have a few months of experience with cardio work, here is another workout that can help you better your cardio capacities while using the concept 2 rowers.

Now, to improve your Aerobic power, you'll have to do the same type of workout but with a shorter burst of higher intensity pushes and rest intervals. One of the most traditional ways is to the original Tabata workouts. There are two different versions. It is basically 4 minutes of HIIT training, 8 sets of 20 seconds at high intensity followed by 10 seconds of lower intensity. If you look at a good and challenging roll session, this could come as close as it gets to what actually happens during a roll. Short bursts of work and a few slower transitions here and there. If it's the first time you try this type of interval training, or can also do 10 seconds of high intensity followed by 20 seconds at a lower intensity, always for 8 sets which come out to 4 minutes in total.

Another simpler and very effective way is to just mimic or even surpass the desired income.

"The more you sweat in training, the less you bleed in combat."
— Richard Marcinko

Let's say you want to be more comfortable at rolling for 5 minutes. Jump on the same rower and go at it for 5 minutes. Check the distance and every single time you go back to it, aim to beat your score. What I often do with my clients is to overshoot the goal. If 5 minutes is the mark, I ask for 6 or 7. I always make the workout worst than the goal so that little 5-minute roll will look like a breeze.

Another piece of equipment that is very efficient to increase cardio capacity is the famous assault bike. Both legs and arms are working together. So for added fun, 30 seconds all out on the assault bike followed by 4 minutes of rolling. You could also use the Tabata protocols on the assault bike as well and to tell you the truth, I find the assault bike way harder than the rower. The difference between the two is that on the rower, I like the pulls which works grip strength and the fact that being crouched up makes it more difficult to breath, which is often the limiting factor when rolling hard. On the other end, the assault bike provides a non-stop, multi-limb workout which brings lactic acid levels through the roof and fast. But great pieces of equipment, you just have to find which one you like or for even better results, make different phases alternating each one of them.

CHAPTER 8

WORKOUT

Now that we discussed some of the most used principles and techniques, let's get into it.

As in BJJ, I decided to have a few options and grade the exercises with different levels of difficulty. Again, in jits, belts are often given with experience which the same goes in weight lifting.

A white belt is usually one for about 1 or 2 years, depending on how many sessions they could get during those years and their own learning curve and injuries.

A blue belt and purple belt could be for about 2 years on average, if not sandbagging to earn more medals in competition or for lack of finding their own path and style.

So in order to follow the same progression path, the exercises in this book will be separated in order of difficulty, white belt would be the easiest to purple the hardest. However, it doesn't mean that a white belt can't do the purple belt exercises. Look at weight lifting the same way as jits, the first year of training you are a white belt. The following two years you are a blue belt in strength and conditioning and move on to purple belt on your fourth and fifth year. To make things easier, all the programs are in actual templates at the end of the book to keep track of your weights.

Phase one would be the rehab/prehab specialization program. Even though you think you might not have any issues structurally, I would advise you to still do this phase. As for the exercises and executions, depending on your level of experience, I would advise you to jump on ExRx.net. They have a great library of both images and videos for all of the following exercises. I reserved a special section for the not so common exercises you might come across in the advanced levels.

Phase 1

For the first phase, we will go into a type of hypertrophy/prehab workout. Hypertrophy is very important when you start training, especially in contact sports since it protects the joints and is a mixture of strength and muscle gains. In Phase one, I use a back offset. Especially for beginners, back offsets are the best when aiming for strength. It improves the ability to use heavier weights and help build in more volume, under fatigue, while keeping a decent technique. For the advanced trainee, being able to train at a higher intensity can have a toll on the nervous system so using this principle can also help the nervous system tolerate additional volume. It can also be a good indicator when a lifter should scale things down or deload. When the athlete is performing a backoff set and experience technical breakdown, it might be an indication that the athlete needs to reduce total volume or give the nervous system a rest.

This study from 2004 compared two sets of lifters, one who performed movements without back offsets and the other with. In a study from The Journal of Strength and Conditioning Researchxx, they found that those who performed a back off set slightly improved their muscular size and strength, while significantly improving their muscular endurance.

In this phase, you will do 3 sets with a weight you can use for 6 to 8 repetitions and add one last set with a weight you can do for 10 reps, which is usually about 20% less than your 6 to 8 rep maximum. Here we go!

White belt phase 1

Phase 1 day 1 upper body

seq	sets	reps	Tempo	rest	Exercise
A1	4	3x6-8, 1x 10	4010	75s	Flat db press
A2	4	3x6-8, 1x 10	4010	75s	Neutral grip pulldown
B1	3	10-12	4010	30s	Seated external rotation on knee
B2	3	12-15	4010	60s	Seated row to collar bone *
C1	4	3x6-8, 1x 10	4010	75s	Low incline db lying extension
C2	4	3x6-8, 1x 10	4010	75s	45' incline curl neutral grip **

*Use a rope and attach it to a seated row pulley. While on a regular seated row pulley, for this one you row to your neck. The most important detail here is to grab the rope with your palms down and with the ball of the rope against your pinky. As you pull the rope up towards your ears with your hands with the palms facing the floor, think about having your elbows going as high as your shoulders.

**Straining the neck is one of the major concerns in this one. As you bring the weight down, keeping the neck on the bench can put some pressure on the cervical spine. Lift your head and look straight in front of you which will elevate the pressure on the cervical area. Keep your elbows pointing down to the floor and curl the weight up.

Phase one day 2 lower body

seq	sets	reps	Tempo	rest	Exercise
A1	4	3x6-8, 1x 10	4010	75s	DB split squat front foot elevated*
A2	4	3x6-8, 1x 10	4010	75s	Lying leg curl
B1	3	8-10	4010	30s	Mixed grip Romanian deadlift**
B2	3	12-15	4010	60s	DB step up (mid calf)
C1	3	10-12	2220	75s	Standing calf raise one legged (no shoes)
C2	3	8-10	4010	75s	QL lift ***

*Elevate your front foot on a step. It could be as high as your lower calf or ankle-high. The goal of this one is to be able to achieve full flexion of the knee, having the back of the leg (hamstring) touch your calf. So if you can't, the higher the front foot, the easier it will be to achieve this goal. As you get a little more flexibility in the hips and ankle, it will get easier and you can lower the front foot's height. The main goal is to do it without the step, straight on the floor.

** mixed grip deadlift allows you to have one hand pronated and the other supinated, taking out the roll of the bar which would tire out the grip while having both hands in a pronated grip. Unless you want to work on your grip, use the pronated grip (both palms facing you).

***also known as side plank.

Those are the most basic versions of exercises to maximize your needs for the sport. The goal is to fix structural issues and progress from there. You can either go to phase 2 of the white belt system or move on to blue belt, keeping the same split.

Depending on the time you allow for training, the 2 days split is best if you can only train a minimum of twice a week. In fact, it would be the absolute minimum if you want to see minimal gains. It could also be a good program in the taper phase.

If you would allow 4 days a week, here is a good way to split it up.

Monday	Tuesday	Wednesday	Thursday	Friday	Saturday	Sunday
Day 1	Day 2	Off	Day1	Day2	Off	Off

For the blue belt system, my goal is to upgrade the exercises to increase the difficulty, always keeping in mind the requirement of our sport. Increasing grip strength, joint stability, and a functional posterior chain. If you have done the white belt workout, this is the logical step forward.

Blue belt phase 1

Phase 1 day 1 upper body

seq	sets	reps	Tempo	rest	Exercise
A1	4	3x6-8, 1x 10	4010	75s	Flat db press fat grips
A2	4	3x6-8, 1x 10	4010	75s	Neutral grip pullups
B1	3	6-8	4010	30s	Seated external rotation on knee (fat grips)
B2	3	10-12	4010	60s	Seated row to forehead, with rope*
C1	4	3x6-8, 1x 10	4010	60s	Flat bench fat grip lying extension DB
C2	4	3x6-8, 1x 10	4010	60s	30 incline db zottman curl **

*Same as the seated row to neck, but your thumbs have to reach your forehead.

** Straining the neck is one of the major concerns in this one. As you bring the weight down, keeping the neck on the bench can put some pressure on the cervical spine. Lift your head and look straight in front of you which will elevate the pressure on the cervical area. For the Zottman version, you curl the weight up with a supinated grip (palms up) and lower the weight with a pronated grip (palms down). However, keep your elbows pointing downwards as you do your pronation.

Day 2 phase 1 lower body

seq	sets	reps	Tempo	rest	Exercise
A1	4	3x6-8, 1x 10	4010	75s	DB split squat *
A2	4	3x6-8, 1x 10	4010	75s	Lying leg curl plantar flexed **

B1	3	8-10	4010	30s	Pronated grip Romanian deadlift
B2	3	12-15	4010	60s	Cyclist squats ***
C1	3	10-12	2220	60s	Standing calf raise one-legged (no shoes)
C2	3	6-8 (or max)	4010	60s	Hanging knee to chest ****(garhammer raise)

There were some small but subtle changes. Using fat grips implements will help increase grip strength.

*Next level from the front foot elevated version. The range of motion should be the same and the goal is to go as far forward as possible while making the hamstring touch the calf without lifting the heel of the front foot.

**Plantar flexed means that your toes are pointing away from your knee, like if your standing up on your toes.

***Put your heels on a platform or on plates, hold the bar behind your butt, squat down while keeping the upper body as perpendicular to the floor as possible.

****hanging from a bar, bring your knee to the chest and as you bring your legs down, don't let them go lower than parallel to the floor.

Purple Belt phase 1

Day 1 mixed

seq	sets	reps	Tempo	rest	Exercise
A1	4	3x6-8, 1x 10	4010	75s	Pronated grip pullups close grip
A2	4	3x6-8, 1x 10	4010	75s	Barbell split squats *
B1	4	3x6-8, 1x 10	4010	75s	Seated row to neck with rope
B2	4	3x6-8, 1x 10	4010	75s	Barbell front squats
C1	3	3x 8-10	4010	60s	Flat bench fat grip lying extension DB
C2	3	3x 8-10	4010	60s	Incline 30' db fat grips pronated grip curl

*Having the barbell on the back puts more emphasis on the glutes and lower back.

Day 2 mixed

seq	sets	reps	Tempo	rest	Exercise

A1	4	3x6-8, 1x 10	4010	75s	Barbell snatch grip deadlift
A2	4	3x6-8, 1x 10	4010	75s	Low incline barbell close grip benchpress
B1	4	3x6-8, 1x 10	4010	75s	Accentuated lying leg curl. *
B2	4	3x6-8, 1x 10	4010	75s	Standing barbell press shoulder width
C1	3	3x 8-10	4010	60s	Toes to bar
C2	3	3x 8-10	4010	60s	Neck bridges on swiss ball

The purple belt phase is an entirely new system since structural issues got taken care of in the first two belts. The major difference in purple is that most exercises give you the most bang for your bucks, big compound lifts.

*This is one of my favorite exercises to increase hamstring strength and to recover bilateral discrepancies. Like a regular leg curl, you lift a weight you can easily curl with both legs (both legs lift 60lbs, 30 pounds on each leg) but do the eccentric portion with only one leg (instantly increases the weight from 30 to 60lbs). For each repetition, you alternate the leg doing the eccentric. So for a total of 8 reps, each leg will lower the weight 4 times.

Phase 2 (8-6-4)x2

This phase will prepare you for the heavier loads you'll have to use in phase three with relative strength/functional hypertrophy. Still on the hypertrophy side which the aim is still to pack a bit of meat on the joints and focus on grip and pulling strength. More volume of work per muscle groups based on a three day split.

Wave loading is tricky but the rewards are well worth it. The way it goes is that the first wave of 8-6-4 is like a pacer to set up the second wave which should be the true 8-6-4 rep maximum. The body sees it as if you are increasing the load continually which always transfers post-tetanic potentiation on the next set. The first time you hit the 4 reps, you trick the body into thinking that it will again need to push heavier weights, though you will have to lower it since you'll have to perform 8 reps again. This simple trick will make you use more weight on the second time around for the second wave! Those who have a good nervous system often use the weight of the 4 reps of the first wave to do 6 on the second wave.

White belt phase 2

Day 1 Chest/back

seq	sets	reps	Tempo	rest	Exercise
A1	6	(8,6,4)x2	3020	90s	Incline benchpress 30° shoulder width
A2	6	(8,6,4)x2	5010	90s	Eccentric pullups *
B1	3	6-8	3020	30s	Standing db shoulder press Unilateral**
B2	3	6-8	3020	60s	One arm bent-over row
C	3	8	4010	75s	mid pulley external rotation

*one of the most important aspects of this workout is the pull-ups. If you can't do 8 pull-ups, start on the lat-pulldown for the recommended reps and go on the pull-ups when you reach the 6 or 4 reps. Even more important is the tempo. To increase strength, the eccentric phase is very important. Go down in 5 seconds (or upon the lat-pulldown) and explode up as fast as possible.

**Unilateral overhead presses engages the core at the same time. If you are working your left arm, put your right foot slightly forward to increase balance.

Day 2 Lower body

seq	sets	reps	Tempo	rest	Exercise
A1	6	(8,6,4)x2	3020	90s	Db squats heels elevated
A2	6	(8,6,4)x2	3020	90s	Lying leg curl Poliquin (eccentric plantar, concentric dorsi flexed)
B1	3	6-8	4010	30s	Low pulley split squats*
B2	3	6-8	4010	60s	Romanian deadlift **
C	3	8	4010	75s	Incline 45' hyperextension

*Grab the pulley with the opposite arm of the working leg. Keep your upper body as straight as possible and both shoulders back.

**Lower back must be as straight as possible to shift the weight/pull on the hamstrings. Some do it with a slight bend in the knees or with the knees completely locked. Try both, use the one you feel which pulls more on the hamstrings.

Day3 Triceps/biceps

seq	sets	reps	Tempo	rest	Exercise
A1	6	(8,6,4)x2	3020	90s	Flat benchpress fat close grip triceps press

A2	6	(8,6,4)x2	3020	90s	Standing barbell curl EZ bar
B1	3	6-8	4010	30s	Flat barbell lying extension ez bar
B2	3	6-8	4010	60s	Scott/preacher bench curl 45' neutral grip DB *
C	3	8	4010	75s	Standing mid pulley One arm row to neck

*on the Scott/preacher bench, the most common mistake is to shift your elbows too far down the bench. Your posture should be as if you were standing up and there should be some space under your armpit and the bench, only leaving the elbow and lowest part of the triceps on the bench. Shoulders should not shifts forward as it puts tremendous pressure on the cervical spine.

White belts are being introduced to fat grips and a small increase in volume. Volume of work means an increase in total sets/reps per workout with an additional day per week.

Here is how the schedule could look like on a 3 day split for all belts.

Option1

Monday	Tuesday	Wednesday	Thursday	Friday	Saturday	Sunday
Day1	Off	Day2	Off	Day3	off	off

Option 2

Monday	Tuesday	Wednesday	Thursday	Friday	Saturday	Sunday
Day1	Day2	off	Day3	off	Day1	Day2
Off	Day3	off	Day1	Day2	off	Day3

Option 3

Monday	Tuesday	Wednesday	Thursday	Friday	Saturday	Sunday
Day1	Day2	Day3	Off	Day1	Day2	Day3
Off	Off	Day1	Day2	Day3	off	Day1

Option one is textbook and the minimum for phase 2. All three options are great, however option 2 and 3 gives less time to rest and regenerate. The volume of work added to rolling sessions can take a toll on the body. Make sure your lifestyle and nutrition are on point to maximize recuperation.

Blue Belt phase 2

Day 1 Chest/back

seq	sets	reps	Tempo	rest	Exercise
A1	6	(8,6,4)x2	3020	90s	Flat db press neutral fat grips
A2	6	(8,6,4)x2	3020	90s	Medium mixed grip pull ups*
B1	3	6-8	3020	30s	Seated barbell front press**
B2	3	6-8	3020	60s	Bent-over barbell row supinated grip
C	3	8	4010	75s	Standing barbell cobra***

*One hand will be pronated and the other supinated. Switch grips for every set (pronated/supinated)

**The seated version engages more than the core since the legs are taken out of the equation.

***Grab a barbell, wider than shoulder grip. Lift your elbows up to shoulder level while keeping the bar close to you. Externally rotate the barbell over your head, always keeping your elbows at shoulder level. Reverse the process to go back down.

Day2 Lower Body/abs

seq	sets	reps	Tempo	rest	Exercise
A1	6	(8,6,4)x2	3020	90s	Barbell back squats
A2	6	(8,6,4)x2	3020	90s	Lying leg curl accentuated plantar flexed toes in*
B1	3	6-8	4010	30s	DB walking lunges
B2	3	6-8	4010	60s	Barbell seated good morning**
C	3	8	4010	75s	Garhammer raise

*Having the toes pointing in (plantar/dorsi flexed) recruits more the Semitendinosus and Semimembranosus. Helps to extend (straighten) the hip joint and flex (bend) the knee joint.

**The Goodmorning has the same goal as the Romanian deadlift, only the bar is on your back. For the seated variation, your legs are stretched out wide in front, feet flat on the floor. With the bar on your back, stick your chest out and try to bring your shoulders down.

Day3 Triceps/biceps/forearms

seq	sets	reps	Tempo	rest	Exercise
A1	6	(8,6,4)x2	3020	90s	Incline benchpress fat grip shoulder width
A2	6	(8,6,4)x2	3020	90s	Scott bench 45' zottman curl*
B1	3	6-8	4010	30s	Decline db lying extension
B2	3	6-8	4010	60s	Incline swiss ball curl neutral grip **
C	3	8	4010	75s	Pronated grip ez bar elbow flexion ***

* on the Scott/preacher bench, your posture should be as if you were standing up and there should be some space under your armpit and the bench, only leaving the elbow and lowest part of the triceps on the bench. Shoulders should not shifts forward as it puts tremendous pressure on the cervical spine. For the Zottman version, you curl the weight up with a supinated grip (palms up) and lower the weight with a pronated grip (palms down). However, keep your elbows pointing downwards as you perform the pronated eccentric phase.

**While lying down on a swiss ball, incline your body at a 45° angle (butt almost touching the floor, stretching down your arms, having your elbows and triceps against the ball. Curl the free weights up while your triceps never lifts off the ball.

***Regular barbell curl with a pronated grip, recruits more the elbow flexors/forearms/ Brachioradialis/Brachialis/Biceps Brachii

Purple belt phase 2

Day1 Chest/back/shoulders

seq	sets	reps	Tempo	rest	Exercise
A1	6	(8,6,4)x2	3020	90s	Flat benchpress close grip low pins *
A2	6	(8,6,4)x2	3020	90s	Side to side wide grips pull ups (left and right

					counts as two reps) **
B1	3	6-8	3020	30s	Swiss ball incline 30° DB fly, supination to pronation ***
B2	3	6-8	3020	60s	One arm Bent-over row to neck
C	3	8	4010	75s	Incline 30' Dumbell powell raise pronated grip ****

*In a squat rack or power rack, set up the safety pins so the barbell rests on the pins 2 inches from your chest. Starting the movement in the stretch position makes it more difficult since you eliminate the stretch reflex as per the conventional benchpress.

**Using a wide pronated grip, pull yourself up side to side. While you pull on one side, try keeping the other arm as straight as possible.

*** Lying down at a 30° angle on a Swiss ball, start with the palms of your hands facing your head (supinated) and as you go down, rotate your hands to stretch out the pecs with a pronated grip with the palms almost facing the floor. As you go back up, slowly turn your hands to a supinated grip tot eh starting position.

****Lying down sideways on a 30° incline bench, Lift your arm up, always keeping it perpendicular to the floor. Keep the hand in a pronated grip throughout the movement. This will work with the traps and posterior shoulder.

Day2 Lower body/abs

seq	sets	reps	Tempo	rest	Exercise
A1	6	(8,6,4)x2	3020	90s	Barbell front squats
A2	6	(8,6,4)x2	3020	90s	Lying leg curl plantar flexed
B1	3	6-8	4010	30s	Barbell lunges *
B2	3	6-8	4010	60s	Glute ham raise **
C	3	8	4010	75s	Russian flag load shifting ***

*Lunges and split squats are different. Lunges are dynamic since you start with both feet together and lunge forward into a split squat, to come back up with both feet back together.

**The glute/ham raise can be done on a specific bench, usually made by Atlantis. If not, kneel on a mat while someone holds your ankles. While keeping the body as straight as possible, lean forward as if you wanted to touch your nose on the floor, to pull yourself back up with your hamstrings. Very hard to perform but doable.

***Russian flags (a la rocky balboa) are best performed on a bench. This version is a step prior to the full-on Russian flags. Lying down and holding the top of the bench, Bring your knees to your chest, extend your legs as high as possible and start going down, keeping your body as straight as a plank, all the way down to the bench.

Day3 Triceps/bicep/forearms

seq	sets	reps	Tempo	rest	Exercise
A1	6	(8,6,4)x2	3020	90s	Triceps dips *
A2	6	(8,6,4)x2	3020	90s	One arm scott bench neutral grip curls **
B1	3	6-8	4010	30s	Low pulley rope lying extension, neutral to pronation ***
B2	3	6-8	4010	60s	Incline 30' db supinated grip curls
C	3	8	4010	75s	Behind the back standing wrist curls barbell

*For triceps dips, cross your legs in the back and shift your upper body forward.

**Very important to keep the same posture as if you were doing both arms.

***Lying down on the floor or on a bench, perform the lying extension with the rope attached to a low pulley. Start in a neutral position and force the wrists to do a pronation as it will be harder with the rope, which is the whole point of the exercise.

Phase   **3**

For the next phase we will dig deeper into the fast-twitch muscle fiber by using a very effective principle called contrast training which uses post-tetanic potentiation (PTP). We will be forcing the muscles into becoming stronger for a few seconds by controlling the speed and choice of exercises we pair together. See it like lifting a half-can of water when you think it's full.

This is by far the most important phase and also, the most taxing, especially if your intent is to keep training and rolling hard. So this program will only be based on a two days split. For best results, use the schedule as shown below;

Option 1

Monday	Tuesday	Wednesday	Thursday	Friday	Saturday	Sunday
Day 1	off	Off	Day2	off	Off	Day 1

Option 2

Monday	Tuesday	Wednesday	Thursday	Friday	Saturday	Sunday
Day 1	off	Day2	off	off	Day 1	off

Not much of a difference but let's say you try phase one to three, the second time around you could try option 2.

My job for this phase is to take moves as close as we can get from BJJ and try to bring strength into the equation. Doing so will give you the ability to transfer the strength qualities you are gaining from all the previous phases into your game. Here we go for the most important phase! Enjoy

White belt phase 3

Day1 Upper body

seq	sets	reps	Tempo	rest	Exercise
A1	4	3-5	3020	30s	Close grip tricep barbell benchpress
A2	4	6-8	10X0	60s	Medicine ball floor throws*
A3	4	3-5	3020	30s	Pull ups neutral grip
A4	4	6-8	10X0	180 s	Med ball or heavy ball slam down**
B	3	8-12	4010	75s	Seated row to neck one arm pronated grip
C1	3	8-12	4010	75s	Dips (feet forward)
C2	3	8-12	4010	75s	Incline zottman curl ***

*lie down on your back and pick a medicine ball of about 20-30lbs for guys and girls should use a 15-20 pounds medicine ball. Throw it 6 times up in the air while lying down on the floor as fast and as explosive as possible.

**A heavy slam ball or bag filled with sand should do the trick. Lift it overhead and slam it down as hard as possible.

*** curl the weight up with a supinated grip (palms up) and lower the weight with a pronated grip (palms down). However, keep your elbows pointing downwards as you perform the pronated eccentric phase.

Day2 Lower body

seq	sets	reps	Tempo	rest	Exercise
A1	4	3-5	3020	30s	DB split squats
A2	4	6-8	10X0	60s	Barbell step up (mid calf level)
A3	4	3-5	3020	30s	Lying leg curl
A4	4	6-8	20X0	180 s	Pull through low pulley *
B1	3	8	4010	75s	DB squat heels elevated
B2	3	8	4010	75s	Unilateral or standing leg curl

*With a rope attached to a low pulley, grab the rope with both hands between your legs and step forward a few feet. Bend over forward as if you were doing a Romanian/stiff legged deadlift. The rope will pull you back, so exploding up is the goal.

Blue belt phase 3

Day1 Chest/back

seq	sets	reps	Tempo	rest	Exercise
A1	4	3-5	3020	30s	Incline bench press 30'
A2	4	6-8	10X0	60s	Medicine ball throws on wall *
A3	4	3-5	3020	30s	Fat grip pull ups (pronated grip) shoulder width
A4	4	6-8	10X0	180s	Med ball or heavy ball slam down **
B1	3	8-12	4010	75s	Flat DB press
B2	3	8-12	4010	75s	Seated row (with Gi, grab collar)

* Stand a few feet from the wall and throw the medicine ball with both

arms. Pay attention to its use and throw it with both arms equally. It's easy to put the ball more on the right hand to push more with the right arm.

**Lift the slam ball overhead and slam it down as hard as possible.

Day 2 Lower body

seq	sets	reps	Tempo	rest	Exercise
A1	4	3-5	3020	30s	Barbell back squats
A2	4	6-8	1010	60s	Prowler sprints (or penta jumps*)
A3	4	3-5	3020	30s	Lying leg curl
A4	4	6-8	10X0	180s	Kettle bell swing
B1	3	15-20	4010	75s	Leg press 45°
B2	3	8-12	4010	75s	Romanian deadlift (stiff legged)

*5 long jumps in a row. Jump as far as possible and spend as little time as possible on the ground in between jumps.

Day 3 Biceps/triceps

seq	sets	reps	Tempo	rest	Exercise
A1	4	3-5	3020	30s	Db close grip tricep press flat
A2	4	6-8	1010	60s	Clapping push ups
A3	4	3-5	3020	30s	Incline db curl 45' (chin up supinated grip purple)
A4	4	6-8	10X0	180s	Heavy ball toss*
B1	3	8-12	4010	75s	Scott bench 45' zottman curl
B2	3	8-12	4010	75s	High pulley towel triceps pushdown

*toss a med ball in the air as high as possible and catch it, spending as little time as possible on your hands.

Purple belt phase 3

Day 1 Chest/back

seq	sets	reps	Tempo	rest	Exercise
A1	4	3-5	3020	30s	Incline db press 30'
A2	4	6-8	10X0	120s	Medicine ball floor throws*
B1	4	3-5	3020	30s	Gi pull ups (collar or spider guard grip)
B2	4	6-8	10X0	120s	Med ball or heavy ball slam down
C1	3	8-12	4010	75s	Flat benchpress low pins

C2	3	8-12	4010	75s	Bent-over barbell row **

*lie down on your back and pick a medicine ball of about 20-30lbs for guys and girls should use a 15-20 pounds medicine ball. Throw it 6 times up in the air while lying down on the floor.

**The upper body must be inclined forward at about 30° from parallel to the floor. Keep the lower back as straight as possible and the knees slightly bent to protect the back.

Day2 Lower body

seq	sets	reps	Tempo	rest	Exercise
A1	4	3-5	3020	30s	Barbell Front squats
A2	4	time	1010	120s	Prowler sprints (or penta jumps)*
B1	4	3-5	3020	30s	Barbell deadlifts
B2	4	10-12	10X0	120s	Kettle bell swing
C1	3	8-12	4010	75s	Barbell split squats
C2	3	8-12	4010	75s	Barbell good morning

*For prowler sprints, push as hard and as fast as possible for about 10 seconds. For penta jumps, the goal is to jump and transition from one jump to the other as fast and as far as possible.

Day 3 Biceps/triceps

seq	sets	reps	Tempo	rest	Exercise
A1	4	3-5	3020	30s	Dips
A2	4	6-8	1010	60s	Deficit jump push ups *
A3	4	3-5	3020	30s	Supinated grip chin ups
A4	4	30 sec	10X0	180s	Gi prowler or sled pulls**
B1	3	8-12	4010	75s	Triceps Frenchpress low pulley
B2	3	8-12	4010	75s	Pronated grip barbell curls

* For this one, you could use 2 bumper plates (big crossfit rubber plates) or 2 small steps, about 2-3 inches from the floor. Start in the push-up position with both hands on the steps on each side. Drop down on the floor and do a push-up. The goal is to push yourself hard enough to bring your hands back on the steps. Focus on speed. When you drop down on the floor, keep going down until your chest touches the floor, don't lock the elbows.

**hook up a gi to a prowler or sled and walk backward while holding the gi sleeves or collars in your hands. Go as heavy as your grip will allow you to support for 30 seconds of work.

That's it !!!

Some might want to add conditioning to their workouts. Although it can help you increase cardio capacity and the obvious health and conditioning attached to it, it can backfire. There is such a thing as training too much, especially if you don't have the caloric intake that goes with it. So let's say you used the Harris-Benedict formula with daily activity adjustment, you could add HIIT or the strongman sessions suggested earlier on.

Rolling will always come first as the primary choice of training to improve cardio capacity, however, you'll be learning how to conserve energy along the way by not training stupid. Some might say that you are using too much strength, some say your cardio sucks, they might be both right. One way or another, you learn and deal with many different styles. So trying to avoid one for the expense of the other is just not reality as you will be rolling with people who are relentless and others that are passive. Having good conditioning will always come in handy.

The next question is; how can I include conditioning in my busy week?

Let's look at some potential scenarios.

If you are weight lifting twice a week plus a 1 or 2 days of rolling, you can add them at the end of your workouts while using the strongman finishers example outlined in chapter 7, or go straight at the end of the book, after the workouts, to see which types of conditioning work could be done at the end of each phase.

If you roll often, prioritize strength training first, rolling in second and maybe 1 or 2 conditioning sessions/finishers at the end of your workouts.

You can also train twice a week and add one long conditioning workout, which is also at the end of this book following the workouts.

If you do weight lifting 3 times a week with at least 2 good rolling sessions, I would suggest adding only 1 or 2 finishers at the end of your workouts. You also have the possibility of splitting your day in two (or three) if time is not an issue. Do your conditioning finishers at the beginning of the day, weight lifting at least 3-4 hours after and rolling in the evening. Needless to say the obvious that having the proper caloric intake during those days is a priority if you don't want to crash and burn.

BLACK BELT

Why didn't I include workouts for the brown and black belts? Why reserve a section especially for the two last belts?

I stumbled on something funny on the ADCC Instagram page recently and it made me think about not only how true it is in jiujitsu, but we can relate in the strength and conditioning field by looking at it with training age and experience.

Here is a little ranked humor.

White belt...you do stupid shit
Blue belt... you quit doing stupid shit
Purple belt...you capitalize on stupid shit
Brown belt... You make people do stupid shit
Black belt...You make people do stupid shit and they don't even know it
Coral belt...You tap people out with whatever stupid shit you want.

If you take a step back and think about the conditioning, training, health aspect of having more than 6 to 8 years of training with jiujitsu, as you grow in the sport, less strength and more techniques come across. You become more intelligent about your game, patient. You actually don't want to use strength. You almost let them do the work for you, capitalizing on mistakes.

As with many sports, the body adapts. It will always follow the road of less effort and with so many years under the belt and as I often hear from the advanced belts, keeping up with the strength and conditioning is often the growing issue, especially if competing.

This section will be prioritizing habits and structural issues/injuries which is the most common denominator for all jiujitsu practitioners. I still haven't heard of someone who never had issues with joints, pain or discomfort during their time on the mats. With that being said, advanced trainees need to realize that there is nothing better than the basics. It will save time and maximize your time in the gym and improve time on the mats. Maybe you did the previous workouts or might be looking to add strength training to your routine for the first time. If you went through the three phases, you'll use these last two phases as a deload, somewhat of a decluttering and reorganizing of the training phases using the best and most time-efficient methods. By the way, for all those who did the previous phases, this section is exactly that. Use these last 2 phases to reorganize and keep progressing.

Basically, as I mentioned before, now is the time to use what will give you the most bang for your bucks, save time, maximize rest and still see improvements on the mats. Now would also be the time to retest and evaluate your progress if you did the first three phases from white to purple. It is also time to think about longevity. Who wouldn't want to roll into their old age?

For example; One of the main components of strength is volume, as in the amount of work per session. Over the years, we accumulate knowledge and experience. This experience allows us to be more effective with our training approach. This experience has also taxed our nervous system, taking a toll on the body.

Hence, you do not need as much training volume to get the same results as you started for several reasons. One is that your recovery abilities gradually diminishes with age. Even if the volume of training is a question of individuality, for strength, between 12 and 16 sessions per month are recommended while for hypertrophy, 16 to 24 sessions per month is the rule.

The duration of your training sessions should not exceed 60 minutes. Long training sessions, no matter how good you feel, borrow energy. You dig into your reserves when your sessions exceed 60 minutes, leading to overtraining or in better words, cumulated fatigue.

One common mistake I see is trying to emulate what the pros do. Don't shoot the messenger but there is a lot of talk on PED (performance-enhancing drugs) which is rampant in the sport. We can't be stupid and ignore this fact or think that it's all good and done naturally. I have nothing against it, to each their own. Assume that what you read may not apply to you.

Many athletes train in different ways and with incredible intensity. Must I also remind you that the majority of these athletes have no children to care for and/or a job that requires a significant workload.

In order to achieve maximum results, invest in a reputable and reliable coach (or this very book) who can bring you a program and/or tips that targets your needs and goals. The return on your investment will be much greater.

I like to stick with the basics, as in using the big lifts and principles. I am 8 to 10 hours in the gym 5 days a week. I also do Jits in our dojo, inside the gym and member in a Gracie Barra where I train for competition. Although I am at my center most of the time, there is not one day that I don't enjoy. I also believe that the secret is that I use my time efficiently. I train for my objectives, my situation, my health, and roll for as long as possible. In order to do so, I learned from my mentor to use my time efficiently and reserve a spot during the day for my passion, which is why my mid-day, is reserve for jits. It keeps me grounded and bumps up my energy again for the rest of the day. When I started jits back again, this is where I also learned that training as much as I did before is not a good idea, and the same went with many of those that I prepared for competition.

It basically comes down to the needs of the individual. You can be a white or black belt, the biggest difference is a white belt will use way more energy than a black belt when rolling with obviously less technique. If you want to lose fat, gain muscle or focus on injury prevention, we all start from the beginning. This is where the testing chapter becomes handy. The first three phases will prepare you for the brown and black belt workouts. Not because it's difficult, but because you gained a certain level of strength, coordination, stamina, cardio vascular endurance, and flexibility. Much like the difference between a white and black belt, the same goes for training experience, hence why the metaphor between training years and jiujitsu belt I used in this book.

After the first three phases, you have become accustomed to strength training, probably gained a fair amount of lean muscle mass and lost fat. Now is the time to move efficiently and with a purpose. The last two phases are what I like to think of the preparation of the rest of your life. You have developed a great strength base, let's widen it and make sure you can roll for as long as you want and even, keep competing at the greatest level.

But here is the thing, let's just say you just earned your brown or black belt and are looking into competing on the biggest stage in the world, the worlds or masters worlds, ADCC or you never know, you get chosen for an invitational like Kasai pro, etc.

Are you physically ready? Most that go compete in these venues go through some type of preparation camp. Top elite athletes such as André Galvao, Romulo Barral and Tom DeBlass go through 10 to 12 weeks of strenuous physical preparation in order to compete because they know that their opponent will do the exact same.

You went through the first three phases and now this is my challenge to you. We will now test your physical abilities beyond the primary testing included in this book. These tests can be used for both beginner (for those who will probably skip to the brown and black belt section thinking they are ready for the challenge) and advanced athletes and specific for BJJ athletes. It challenges both physical and skills components, like the stand-up game as well as skills under pressure and elevated heart rate which can mess things up big time in competition due to fast lactic acid build-up.

Under IBJJF rules, these are the matches times ranked by belts

	adult	masters
white	5min	5
Blue	6	5
purple	7	6
brown	8	6
black	10	6

I wanted this challenge to reflect all the components of an actual competition fight as close can be. This test is performed with 10 stations done consecutively, alternating skills that challenge defensive/offensive components and physical/strength and conditioning skills.

Furthermore, these tests were put together in a matter that replicates competition settings. Stress, as seen in the energy system chapter, can challenge metabolic and cardiovascular output so this is why I start the challenge with something that raises the heart rate quickly and efficiently for the sport. There will be two proposed challenges. One that could be done in a dojo without the use of equipment and I will include the one I use at my facility with all the recommended equipment and I'll do my best to add some alternative, although it might change the norms but can be useful for coaches and athletes to at least get some baseline norms for their dojo/team.

For the dojo challenge, you will need one or two good drilling partner that is about the same weight and height. If you can't have someone who has greater skills or is of higher belt than you to ensure validity and efficiency of techniques, have someone supervise you. The goal is to keep the technique and efficiency while under pressure and fatigue close to perfection. Having a few people from the team perform the test makes it more interesting and this is what I call team building[9].

Dojo challenge

10 station BJJ specific challenge for dojo	
station	Skill/physical
1	10 burpees(start with chest on floor, do a push-up, knee to chest, squat up to jump, squat down knee to chest, extend the legs back to start position with chest on the floor, 1 down, 9 to go)
2	2 Double leg take down each side
3	5 clapping push-ups (arms start at below 90°, push up explosively to clap, repeat 10 times)
4	2 technical get up each side
5	15 sit-ups (partner holds feet, start with full back on the floor and hands/fingers crossed behind the head, elbows have to touch the knees to count)
6	2 three brothers drill (closed guard to arm bar to omoplata to triangle) each side
7	10 walking lunges each leg (knee has to gently touch the ground to count)
8	2 kase gatame escapes each side
9	10 Gi supine pull-ups with partner (partner is standing up over your hips, grab the sleeves of both partner's arms, keeping the leg straight, pull yourself up, fully extending the arms on the way down)
10	Mount to back take drill 2 each side

I strongly suggest that you review each drill before the test since the goal is to complete the challenge for a given time, so have a good review and

[9] For the coaches, here is one little tip. After the team went through the challenge, post the scores and divide the team according to the best times. Let's say you have 6 guys, team A would be the first two best, Team B would be 3rd and 4th and so on. Team A would get all the perks. So in order to get in team A, you have to beat one of them scores. Put a little motivation for team B and C and Team A can't grab their asses if they want to stay on top. Puts a little oil on the fire and fires up the whole dojo. Enjoy the rolls!

make sure you perform them the best you can. However, the goal is to roll them under pressure, fatigue, stress and that is the ultimate goal, roll your best, built-in technique under fatigue and stress.

Gym/dojo challenge

If you are fortunate enough to have a dojo with a gym included in it

station	Skill/physical
1	Max watts/max time - assault bike/rower/skierg
2	2 Double leg take down
3	Barbell deadlifts bodyweight x5
4	4 guard replacement from side control
5	5 toes to bar
6	2 three brothers drill (from guard, arm bar to omoplata to triangle)
7	5 barbell front squats with 10 RM
8	10 ashi garamis each side (no sweep, drill side to side continuously)
9	5 pullups neutral grips (full range, from straight arm to chin over bar)
10	Mount to back take drill 1 each side

10 station BJJ specific challenge for dojo with GYM

For these two variations of the BJJ specific tests, a time of 5 minutes is the goal. But to tell you the truth, it is somewhat irrelevant as a lot of elements can change the average. Maybe someone could be good at techniques but fail to perform the strength qualities required. Maybe the conditioning is the missing link to your game. That is exactly what these tests were created for. First, as a marker of overall strength and conditioning. They could also provide a lot of information about your current conditioning, especially if you are looking into competing or just improving your game.

Take note of the time you made, and aim at improving it next time around. Yes, the goal would be to get near or under the 5-minute mark, but for this test, you are your own opponent. Improving your skills, strength, conditioning, will make you gain time and efficiency under pressure. Aim at perfecting your technique, keeping a great pace and being strong under pressure.

Knowing is half the battle. Organizing the next phase and the approach is the other half. Strength/conditioning and jits might have something in common. When comes the time to plan a workout or to fight, the more experience you have, the more tools you have at your disposition right?

As you gain experience in jiujitsu, judo or wrestling, you know your game plan, your weaknesses, and strengths. While rolling you have many options and choose them accordingly. You won't spend time with crazy shit and focus on what needs to be done and use what you know can get you the win without crazy efforts.

The same goes for strength and conditioning. As you get older, you know what works or not for you if you have been training steadily long enough. You obviously know your strengths and weaknesses. These tests were made to let them shine.

Even though you might already be a brown or black belt, if you haven't already gone through the first 12 weeks phases as a white to purple training belt (in training), I would greatly advise you to do so. You can even try the initial tests at the beginning of this book if you haven't done it already and use them as strength and health markers.

For these next two phases, we will work on strength/speed/power. It is the logical step forward after you have done the first 12 weeks. You have gained quite a bit of strength, so let's look at transferring it further into that rabbit hole that is speed/strength and power development.

Brown belt phase

This workout was created by one of my mentors, André Benoit. One of the best strength coaches in the strength and conditioning world, he also participated in the 88 and 92 Olympics in the sport of Luge. Using his own experience as an elite athlete, he went on to train others including:
The Canadian Alpine Ski Team, luge, skeleton, bobsleigh, and speed skating teams. Top NFL, CFL, Track and Field, and NHL Athletes.

Andre is a Poliquin Level 5 coach (Highest attainable level. Must train an Olympic Medalist in order to become level 5). He has also worked directly with the world-renowned Charles Poliquin for almost two decades.

In this phase, we dig in work capacity, volume and strength. Short rest interval with 80-85% of your 1 rep max. We basically give this type of workout to take someone out of a training plateau. Although more of a bodybuilding style, the main focus is to gain strength endurance as well as gaining strength and lean muscle tissue.

Day 1

seq	sets	reps	Tempo	rest	Exercise
A1	4	6-8	3010	30s	30°Incline db press
A2	4	6-8	3010	30s	Seated row to neck with rope
B1	5	2-4	3010	120s	Flat benchpress
B2	5	2-4	3010	120s	Neutral grip pull ups
C1	6	6-8	4010	30s	Low incline db fly (10-20°incline)
C2	6	6-8	4010	30s	One arm bent-over row

Day 2

seq	sets	reps	Tempo	rest	Exercise
A1	4	6-8	3010	30s	DB split squats
A2	4	6-8	3010	30s	Romanian deadlift
B1	5	2-4	3010	120s	Barbell squats
B2	5	2-4	3010	120s	Lying leg curl
C1	6	6-8	4010	30s	hyperextension
C2	6	6-8	4010	30s	Standing calf raise

Day3

seq	sets	reps	Tempo	rest	Exercise
A1	4	6-8	3010	30s	Barbell lying extension
A2	4	6-8	3010	30s	Pronated grip medium ez bar curl
B1	5	2-4	3010	120s	Close grip triceps barbell benchpress
B2	5	2-4	3010	120s	Standing barbell curl
C1	6	6-8	4010	30s	Low pulley rope frenchpress
C2	6	6-8	4010	30s	Scott bench 45° DB neutral grip curl

Use the A1-A2 superset to gradually ramp up the weight. See it as a gradual warmup. Let's say you know you can use 100 pounds on the bench press, start with 60 lbs on the first set, second set 75 lbs, 85-90 lbs on the third and near or max on the last set. The following week, you can start with 70 pounds, and so on. This should be done at almost every workout.

Black belt phase

This method is one of my favorites to build pure strength and was popularized by none other than Jim Wendler. The 5-3-1 is based on the principle of strength building with the core lifts, such as the bench press, squats, deadlifts, and overhead press. However, in this case and to keep it sport-specific. We will also add in some remedial/assistance work for injury prevention, keep on building muscles and create balance between the structure and the musculature.

Although this workout doesn't seem like a lot of work, working near 90-100% of your 1 RM takes a toll on the nervous system so it is possible to use this method with a 3 or a 4 days split. I'll use a 4 day split in this case while using BJJ specific exercises, which obviously won't stray very far from the basic multi joints lift.

Day 1

seq	exercise	Sets/week	reps	Tempo	rest	% 1 RM
A	benchpress	3 sets		3010	180	
		Week 1	5			65,75,85%
		Week 2	3			70,80,90%
		Week 3	5,3,1			75,85,95%
		Week 4	5			40,50,60%
B	Standing shoulder press	5	8-10	3010	90s	
C	Bent-over barbell row	5	8-10	3010	90s	

Day 2

seq	exercise	Sets/week	reps	Tempo	rest	% 1 RM
A	Barbell deadlift mixed grip	3 sets		3010	180	
		Week 1	5			65,75,85%
		Week 2	3			70,80,90%
		Week 3	5,3,1			75,85,95%
		Week 4	5			40,50,60%

| B | Lying leg curl unilateral | 4 | | 8-10 | 3010 | 90s | |
| C | Hanging leg raise | 5 | | 8-10 | 3010 | 90s | |

Day 3

seq	exercise	Sets/week	reps	Tempo	rest	% 1 RM
A	Pull ups	3 sets		3010	180	
		Week 1	5			65,75,85%
		Week 2	3			70,80,90%
		Week 3	5,3,1			75,85,95%
		Week 4	5			40,50,60%
B	Standing barbell press	5	8-10	3010	90s	
C	Seated external rotation on knee	4	8-10	3010	90s	

Day 4

seq	exercise	Sets/week	reps	Tempo	rest	% 1 RM
A	Back squats	3 sets		3010	180	
		Week 1	5			65,75,85%
		Week 2	3			70,80,90%
		Week 3	5,3,1			75,85,95%
		Week 4	5			40,50,60%
B	DB split squats	4	8-10	3010	90s	
C	Lying leg curl	5	8-10	3010	90s	

As you can see, very simple programming but one of the most effective programs I have came across. Remember that you're calculating percentages based on 90% of your current 1RM in each lift, not from the actual 1RM. If you want to know your 1 rep max, even though you never tried to max out before, go on repmaxcalc.com. to have an average. Remember that 1 rep max percentages are never an exact science and can vary greatly from one week to another.

Strength is the mother of all qualities. Using these compounds lifts work the body as a whole. They bring strength qualities you can transfer on the mats and to any sports for that matter. You gain the type of strength qualities that are functional. The muscles should work as a chain of command. Each one has a specific goal, and they all have to interact in a given way to support one or more muscles for a given movement. Our bodies are complex machines that need some taken care of, understanding the intricate inner functions and abilities we gain by getting stronger can only help our game in so many ways.

PLANIFICATION AND PERIODIZATION

Failure to plan is planning to fail

You can have all the talent in the world but preparation is the key to success, without a shadow of a doubt. For now, you have a fairly detailed plan on how you could gain strength to better your game. You can, with a little effort, create your year in advance. Life will always throw you curve balls, like injuries, family issues, work-related delays, and problems, etc. So having the perfect plan is practically impossible, but having a plan also includes being able to readjust accordingly, dodging the bullets à la Neo in Matrix-style.

Enter periodization

Let's take a full calendar year and write down all the competition you would like to do. 1, 2, 4, whatever. Even if you are not contemplating the competition thrill, I would suggest you plan at least a few months ahead of time some of your workouts and roll sessions. One of the major mistakes I see is people who are all out and never take pauses or breaks. No, they don't make you weaker and no you won't be missing out.

Even the best cars in the world, if you always put the pedal to the metal, will break down eventually or you'll crash and burn. This is an unwanted break which could be longer than you would like too. The same goes for your body. You can't always keep training and not expecting something to go wrong. Sure, there are some lucky bastards out there who roll 2-3 times a day. I know a few of them, but they always end up with nagging pains and then, you don't see them for a couple of months because of this stupid little nagging injuries that became much worst because they didn't want to stop.

Periodization is all that put together and if there is one section in this book that you would not want to go over is this one. Failure to plan is planning to fail.

Let's take someone who would like to get 2 competition in the span of 8 months. Here is what a very simple plan would look like.

Jan	Feb	March		April	May		June	July		august
str	hyp	str	DL	comp	trans	hyp	str	hyp	DL	comp

10 weeks are for the preparation phase and the last 2 weeks are reserved for the specific preparation phase when they usually roll more and cut down on gym time (DL = deload/tapering, which will be more in detail in the competition chapter). The first preparation phase from January to March had a higher percentage of strength work than the second phase before the august competition.

Most periodization charts and plan always alternate phases of high intensity and volume. Like I mentioned earlier, the intensity is inversely proportional to volume so alternating is required to prevent overtraining and saving the joints of the constant beating of high-intensity weight lifting.

Depending on the qualities to be acquired, one that needs to gain strength will obviously spend a little more time in the gym with a strength training protocol (as the previous example), which would be the same as for someone who is looking to gain more size with hypertrophy.

After the first competition, there is a transition phase, more like a rest and regeneration phase which I and most veterans strongly suggest. It's not complicated, just common sense. Then again, depending on your goals, calendar year, the outcome and design of the plan could be a lot different, so to each their own. What you have now is a simple way to plan your workouts ahead of greater things to come.

CHAPTER 9

COMPETITION PREP

This is, in fact, the most critical part of the process. The big steps towards competitions. The first competition is probably going to be the worst experience ever. Then, you'll be able to better manage the nerves, but still, the nervousness while never go away completely.

Is there a way to prepare for it? No way. The best way to describe it is to imagine your heart being somewhat alert to 100 miles an hour.

You are in a completely unknown territory, so stress levels are unusually high. You don't want to look dumb, or you don't want to get beaten, to show that you don't give up easily. This type of response will dig deep into your central nervous system.

"Survival factors affected by the CNS system"

• Once activated, the CNS pushes the heart rate from its normal level of 60-80 bpm to more than 200 bpm in seconds.

• The optimal range for a combat performance is between 115-145 bpm

After 115 bpm, dexterity begins to deteriorate
At 145 bpm, complex motor skills begin to deteriorate and judgment begins to be affected. Ex: reaction time to potentially dangerous situations.
At 175 bpm, the only physical actions you can control are the overall motor abilities. (crawling, running and climbing)

You will quickly go to the last level, 175 and up. You'll probably gas out, unable to use strength to get out, or just grab something since your grips will give out...

Unfortunately, that's only in the first minute or so. You still have 4 minutes ahead of you.

Another huge detail you need to consider some points. While training in the competition class, a few times, you'll hear your coach yell "you got your points". They will even have a few classes when they tally the points as you roll. If you had the pleasure to experience a few rolls like that, put that same stress level 1000.times.

One of the most common mistakes when preparing for competition is timing. If you don't take it seriously, even for advanced trainees and players, you'll end up gassing out quickly. It is also quite possible. This is where the timing and a little help from an experience coach can come-in handy.

I'll leave what you do on the mats to your BJJ coach. As you will be drilling endlessly your game plan, and standup fighting maybe a month or more before the comp, your body will take a beating. Since everything puts a toll on your body, I would advise you to cut down on the training volume instead of stopping completely.

The art of peaking

Sometimes, magic happens. Like all magicians, some tricks are up their sleeves and it is a well-kept secret only known amongst the magician's guild.
As a strength coach, you must understand a very intricate principle that has the ability to bring the best out of your athletes when they need it the most.

The principle of peaking.

Imagine getting up on the day of the competition, well-rested and fired up. Like if all the perfect conditions for the perfect storm had all came together to create the storm of the century. As if someone pissed off Zeus. You have trained and dieted for months to get to a given weight, to be able to land those Ippons and drilling your game plan. You can't afford to mess things up on the day you need it the most.

This is why it is of the utmost importance to get your shit right and not just rely on luck or "we'll see what happens when we get there." kinda plan. Having a plan helps you get to the destination safely, increases the chances of getting in top conditions at the right time and mostly, writing down everything you did to get there helps you keep track of every little detail. Once all is said and done, you can analyze it all and see what went wrong so you don't repeat the same mistakes again.

Enter the art of peaking.

Peaking, which is the ultimate goal of periodization, the process that leads to achieving the best performance at competition day. For peaking correctly, we use the principle of tapering, also known as deloading. It is the way to reduce the accumulation of training fatigue by lowering progressively or drastically the training volume prior to a competition or a given event to improve one's performance. It is in fact, the final phase prior to a major competition.

Coaches have relied on this principle for years, almost exclusively by trial and error. Unfortunately, trying to narrowing it to a simple technique or given the program and yell EUREKA is far fetched. Coaches have used the shotgun approach too often, meaning that they put all kinds of principles and ideas into the program which makes it very difficult to narrow it down to specific elements that bring us results.

In my opinion, all the phases are very important in a periodization protocol, however, if the taper is done efficiently, everything that was done prior to it will come in full effect when the time is crucial.

The culmination of a strength coach's career is that exact moment. Being able to bring their athletes to the best of his abilities at the exact moment you need them to.

However, not all athletes react the same and in the same manner during the taper. This is why there is no perfect way. There will always be a need to individualize periodization and most certainly the taper phase as there are physiological and psychological aspects to take into account.

When planning the taper phase, you need to know how long, and in what manner you will eliminate accumulated fatigue but still continue to adapt to training. The most challenging and individual aspect of the taper is the duration. Bosquet and colleagues (2007) found that the taper should last between 8 to 14 days prior to gain all the benefits from fatigue withdrawal and the negative effects of detraining (loss of performance and strength).

It seems like 2 weeks is the norm for all sports as taper duration. However, tapering is not meant to cut down completely on training. You can reduce the volume of training by as much as 60% depending on the individual. You can also bring it down gradually or drastically. I find that the drastic method is best, especially if you are in the last week's prior competition. While the training volume is lessened, more emphasis should be put on technique, rehab/prehab, and visualization.

As an example, if your weight training protocol gives you 4 sessions a week and you roll 5-6 days a week, I would advise to do 1-2 weight lifting session and doing 60% of the usual volume, keeping the necessary into the plan and for the rolls, 4 per week while practicing your game plan.

The art of winning

My interest from martial arts came very early in my life and one of the very first books I bought with my own money was The art of war from Sun Tzu.

After reading many versions of it, relating to the business or other aspects of our lives, I've used it in combat, business and also built a version of it towards strength training.

Here are a few quotes that had a great impact on my life, training, and habits.

"So in war, the way is to avoid what is strong, and strike at what is weak. To know your Enemy, you must become your Enemy."

In combat, this cannot be any clearer. But in training, most people will avoid their weaknesses. You are your own worst enemy in training, always fighting that little voice in your head trying to make you do less then you are supposed to.

Most fighters study their opponents before the big fight. You must apply the same principle before every workout, before making your programs. You know your weaknesses so don't let them define your strength.

In the gym, one of the best ways to crush your weak points is to train with a stronger partner. Your ego will probably get a beating as well, but if your ego is more important than getting bigger and stronger, I can tell why you have such weaknesses.

"To be prepared beforehand for any contingency is the greatest of virtues."

As we study our opponents, we also know the date of the dual, the big fight. We have only one thing in our mind, the ultimate fight night.

In training, we set goals so we don't waste our precious time. The best trainers always have a plan B. Injuries, planning mistakes and what we call "life" happens and can throw curve balls to the best of us no matter how well the plan goes so being prepared for any eventualities is in fact, the greatest virtue.

"If the mind is ready, the body will follow without any great effort."

Your state of mind has a lot to do with your practice. The ultimate goal of all martial artists has the perfect practice. That is when technique meets the mind and the ultimate outcome is extreme fluidity and effortless execution. The best way to visualize such a thing is in the movie Matrix when Neo realizes that he is the chosen one and easily executes all the techniques he learned, effortlessly against the agents, with extreme fluidity and agility.

There will be some moments in your workout and practice, where you will find it easier, more fluid. Almost like a déjà vu kind of feeling, like something you already experienced before which we perceive as easier and known territory. I've read many times in old martial ways writings, the perfect practice, and some kind of moment of enlightenment.

I have had the pleasure of experiencing a few of these moments which were not planned, and I think they never do. This is why it makes them so special and why the ultimate goal is to experience them as often as possible through constant practice and study of our ways.

Everything seemed almost too easy, automated and even slower than usual, almost as if I knew what was coming my way and had all the time in the world to react and conquer. I controlled the situation and how I reacted to it. A great fighter can almost follow the opponents breathing and hit at the right moment. The best way to explain the feeling is like having a perfect balance between mental, physical and spiritual capacities, a perfect balance between memory, technique, and execution.

In training, we can have a little more control over our abilities by keeping track of our progress. There will be workouts where everything seems easier. A training journal will have many relevant details about those greater workouts and may have many answers to how you can maximize your results for the upcoming programs and workouts.

"Victorious warriors win first *and then go to war, while defeated warriors go to war first and then seek to win."*

You know how to achieve the best practice. Fighting will be much easier and so are your workouts. Cry in the dojo, laugh in the battlefield.

"Know yourself, and your enemy, a thousand battles, a thousand victory."

The best of the best always study their opponents before the big fight. They will use their strengths and weaknesses wisely.

In training, the same goes for our own weaknesses and strongest abilities and this goes in many areas of our lives. For instance, your schedule may not allow you to train more than 4 times a week. Overlooking this simple but very important detail may impact your ability to recuperate and may cause great damage to your health in the long run.

Follow the wave and be realistic. Nothing is temporary. Don't risk it all for the sake of pride. Use these periods to rest and reassess.

For those who burn the candle from both ends, having a few tricks up your sleeve can help you come back faster from those sleepless and restless nights induced by overbooked schedules. Magnesium will help calm your nervous system down and ease your mind. Working late at night on that bright blue computer screen may have a part in it, messing up your body's perception of sleep so melatonin and magnesium can help improve your sleep quality.

"In the midst of chaos, there is also opportunity."

I was very fortunate to have a sensei that challenged me relentlessly. I wish you the same in your practice, in the dojo, and in the gym. Get someone to do your workouts. In fact, your workouts should scare you a little, make them challenging. No one in the history of mankind complained about being too strong.

"A leader leads by example, not by force."

This one is for all the "show off". You are a strong dude? There might be a few who are looking up to you, they want to do what you do and they would kill to have your skills and/or strength. You have the power to influence the next generation so do it correctly.

There were always those little self-proclaimed alphas that came in the class who thought they were able to fight with the best of us. Techniques, skills, and methods can only be tested in combat. This is where experience count. Knowledge and composure will prevail. These are the type of situations where the students learn the most from the sensei.

"Strategy without tactics is the slowest route to victory. Tactics without strategy are the noise before defeat."

The best tactic is to use an unfair advantage. Discover the weakest link and use it to your advantage. Use techniques that will make you reach your goals faster. They won't be the easiest, they never are, but then again, they will help you gain the advantage.

This is the exact reason why some need to focus on conditioning, on strength, or just improve overall health.

"Swift as the wind. Quiet as the forest. Conquer like the fire. Steady as the mountain."

Control the elements.

When fight day comes, wouldn't it be stupid to eat like you didn't care? To sleep only a few hours? So in training. It could be one of the most expensive lessons you can learn. Eat and live as if you were going to be tested every day.

"He who knows when he can or can not fight, will be victorious."

One must learn when to calm down, to take it easy, rest and restore, take a break from practice and training. This is where the efficacy of the periodization principle lies. Our body (and obsessive propensities) does not always recognize the early symptoms of overtraining. Many would want us to believe that overtraining is just an excuse for the weak, but that would be their weakness. Know when to ease off the accelerator and throughout the year, plan periods of rest, regeneration and refocus. You don't have to wait until you crash and burn, keep progressing by implementing this principle. This will prevent many overuse injuries and will add many more years to your practice.

CHAPTER 10

SUPPLEMENTATION

Supplements are exactly what the word is intended to be. It is and should always be a supplement to what your actual nutrition will provide. Why should you need a supplement then if your diet provides you with all you need?

Basically, the answer to this is as simple as understanding that the quality of the food we eat is not as good is it once was. With all the food regulation policies and the quality of the soil just to name a few issues makes it harder for us to get anywhere near our true nutritional requirements, especially for those of us who have a very active lifestyle.

There is also the question of genetics. Some of us have won the lottery and can get away with anything. They can eat whatever they want and still look good, with no health issues whatsoever. May they be young or old, one day, it will catch up. There are also those who weren't that lucky with the genetic Russian roulette and got a few issues that their genes always keep reminding them that no matter how good they do, they have to walk the line very tightly.

Now, even if you are blessed with good genes, I would strongly advise you consider taking what I consider the basics in which I believe can provide you the nutritional requirement of what the active population should take to be able to function properly and be able to enjoy their favorite activity and enjoy it for as long as they desire. What follows is what I usually suggest to my clients and athletes, in order of importance. No supplements should be taken without proper consultation with your physician or qualified health practitioner. The following supplement shave proven their efficiency on the general and active population but the principle of individuality is always a priority. Before you start taking any type of supplements, please consult and make sure that any supplement is right for you and can be mixed with any medication you might be taking at the moment.

The basic supplements are to provide what the body requires to function optimally. Cell regeneration is the main goal when it comes to healthy nutrition, and with specific supplementation, the process can be optimized. The fact that the active population puts the body through higher stress [10] than a couch potato is a no brainer why we need more nutrients.

For anyone, active or not, my go-to supplement in priority are; **fatty acids a.k.a. omega 3's a.k.a. fish oils**. Fatty acids, which are long chains of carbon, are classified as saturated, monounsaturated and polyunsaturated. Polyunsaturated fats contain omega-3s and omega-6s. However, Americans consume 10 times more omega-6s (pro-inflammatory) than omega-3s (anti-inflammatory). A healthier ratio would be 1:1 instead of the 1:20 with today's food reality.

For us elite athletes, the benefits are numerous. Fish oil supplementation leads to attenuated oxidative stress in response to strenuous exercise. This is positive in that it reduces exercise-induced inflammation, decreases delayed-onset muscle soreness and increases the rate of recovery. Other well-known benefits are[xxi];

- Fish oil induces fat breakdown while sparing glucose/glycogen.
- In most of the studies, fish oil increased cardiovascular health even if performance was not enhanced to a statistically significant degree.
- Fish oil supplementation has been associated with improving cognitive abilities including reaction time, decision making, and stabilizing mood.

Few people see great results from taking omega 3's because they don't take enough. All the research has been done on fairly unhealthy individuals and with doses as high as 10gr. Per day. Here is the logic behind what should be done. The fatter you are, the more you need. The fact is that if you are categorized as obese, your cellular membrane is probably not as healthy is it should. Omega 3's are key for the health of the cell membrane, it promotes the fluidity and integrity of the membrane. Too much-saturated fat and the integrity of the membrane go out the door and nothing gets in. This wall, when equipped the right amount of the good fatty acids, lets the nutrients into the cells and waste products get out. It provide a protective barrier, they don't let everything in, especially large particles. Cell membranes also release fatty acids when the body needs it, such as for growth or dealing with an injury. If these mechanisms are defective,

---

[10] Even though activity is a good stress, if you don't manage it well with the proper nutritional and supplement protocol, damage can be done to the body in many ways.

declining health is obviously an issue. So providing a healthy source of fatty acid such as fish oil is essential to reverse the damage.

I go with body composition. The higher your body fat percentage is, the higher the dose. If you have a 20% body fat, which means that 20% of your weight is adipose tissue a.k.a. FAT, you should take 20gr. of fish oil per day. Yes, it's a lot, but the research uses these guidelines as well. As you get healthier, and your body fat percentage goes down, so does your fish oil dosages. On a very important side note, I would start by bringing up the dosage slowly as in start with 5-6 gr. Per day and go up. I have seen lots of great results with half the dosage and always aim for pharmaceutical grade supplement companies. Look for GMP certification (good manufacturing products).

Next up are the **multivitamins.**

For multi's, most people don't see them as necessary, and this might be true for the general population who are not active. But I've seen it times and times again that as soon as one starts taking a good quality multivitamin a day, how they seem to feel a little better. You shouldn't feel like a big difference. What the multi's provide the bare minimum of the nutrients so if you know you are lacking in the nutrition side for whatever reasons, I highly recommend them. For us active population, it's fairly easy to say that even though we stick with the nutrition plan, we often end up missing a few meals to provide enough of the nutrients and calories our body needs. So multi's can help. Even if your diet is on point, maybe some digestive issues or genetic default set you up with some nutrient deficiency, so a multi can make sure you get the bare minimum of what you might need.

One of the major complaints we see is cramps.

The next big issue for jujitsu is **joint support**. What I like about fish oils is that they help in many ways which supporting the joints is one of them. The help, even more, join integrity you can take

On a very important last note, **no supplement can ever replace or let alone work optimally without the help of a great nutrition plan and a healthy lifestyle.**

I am lucky enough to have a team to work with. One of which is great and in my opinion the best supplement company for sports and performance. Here is Vincent Comtois, vice president ATP Lab: Athletic-Therapeutic-Pharma.

"When it comes to supplementation and performance, especially for combat athletes, it is important to have the specific needs of the athlete in mind.

Combat sports have common denominators: strength, power, and endurance. So, in terms of supplementation, all fighters have similar needs whether it be a boxer or a Jujitsu player. The goal that remains is to adjust the dosages, the frequency, according to the individual needs of the athlete.

It seems very clear that Nutrition remains the foundation of everything, for both health and performance. However, it is very difficult to meet the very high nutritional needs of an athlete without supplementation. The level of energy and expenditure, perspiration, as well as the training frequency poses a great challenge to the athlete wishing to perform at his best without a big weight fluctuation, which is a very important aspect of combat sports.

There is also the famous "weight cut" which represents in itself a colossal challenge. Losing a big deal of weight, without diminishing the ability to perform, requires precise calculations that cannot be left to chance. What follows is what I think the ideal supplementation formula for the combat athlete.

The key to performance is first and foremost, optimal health. This might look like a very simple observation but many athletes or even worse, their coach, often relegates health to second place.

We often look at macronutrients like protein, carbs and fats but how about the micronutrients, they are often the most common deficiencies.

Poor food sources, cooking and less then desirable conservation are all factors that deplete foods of its micronutrient contents.
So nowadays, supplements are essential not only for athletes but also everyday people.

Multivitamins

This complex of vitamins and minerals acts as an insurance policy as micronutrition for the athlete. The balanced diet should bring the essential and the "multi" offers optimality. As synthetic vitamins of poor quality can be more counterproductive than helpful, the quality of the product is very important.

So to have a good "multi", you have to make sure that it includes so-called "active" B-complex vitamins, chelated minerals, etc. A multivitamin sold in pharmacies, one tablet a day at $ 15, it's more or less a balm for people who can't afford it and want to feel good. No multivitamin can provide the daily dose required with less than four capsules a day. Plan to pay more, and consider it a real investment for your health and long-term health.

Omega-3

If your diet contains a lot of processed products and your meat does not come from organic farms fed on pasture, your diet will be high in omega-6 and low in omega-3. The ideal ratio between omega 6 to omega 3 is 4:1. The average American eats a ratio of anywhere from 12:1 to 25:1 omega 6 to omega 3. Such a high ratio tremendously increases the chances of health problems and promotes inflammation.

Avoid canola oil, margarine, soybean oil, safflower oil, sunflower oil, and any other vegetable oils. These types of oils are too fragile and can't sustain the heat especially when you cook with them. They become rancid very fast. Note that linseed, chia, hemp, pumpkin seeds, and walnuts are good sources of short-chain ALA and should be part of a healthy diet. It is necessary however to be aware that the conversion rate to EPA and DHA is low and even very difficult for some people.

Oily fish is an excellent source of EPA and long-chain DHA, mainly salmon, herring, mackerel, trout, and sardines. Some blue/green algae contain also EPA and especially DHA and represent the source of the food chain.

If you decide to use supplements, choose a supplement in an opaque bottle. Source omega-3 must come from small fish such as herring, mackerel, sardines and/or anchovy. The oil must be filtered and distilled to ensure a minimum of heavy metals, pesticides, and PCBs. Some companies will push even further by adding vitamin E that serves as an antioxidant and protects fatty acids against oxidation. Some companies decide to attach fatty acids to a triglyceride to improve absorption and to get closer to what nature is already providing us.

In summary, omega-3s have an anti-inflammatory effect since they come to help or restore balance with the omega-6s that are present in larger quantities in our diet. Fatty acids such as omega-3's promote a good fluidity of our cell membranes, improving communications between the outside and inside of the cells which are essential for good health and good performance sports.

Magnesium

Magnesium is present in every cell in our body and is involved in more than 300 enzymatic and biochemical reactions, including energy production. Magnesium is necessary to maintain our bone density and good sugar management, as well as to ensure normal heart rhythm and normal lung function.

It is very difficult to detect magnesium deficiency. Unfortunately, even a blood test does not give enough clues since only 1% of magnesium is found in the blood, which does not detect a deficiency at the cellular level. Dr. Norman Shealy, a well-known neurosurgeon in the United States said, "All known diseases have a characteristic of magnesium deficiency ". In Canada as in the United States, it is estimated that about 60% to 70% of people do not consume the minimum daily dose (RDA = recommended daily allowance). Several experts agree that the RDA is too low for most nutrients. If we recommended a dose closer to what is considered optimal, the rate of deficiencies would probably exceed 85%.

As the consumption of dairy products is high and the consumption of vegetables is insufficient, the ratio between calcium and magnesium is imbalanced in many people.

Ideally, we should aim for a ratio that is close to 1:1, while the current ratio is more 5 to 1 and can go up to 15 to 1. The ratio is important and it is unbalanced by a lack of magnesium more than a surplus of calcium. An unbalanced ratio is involved in conditions such as migraines, ADD / ADHD, autism, fibromyalgia, anxiety, asthma, PVM (mitral valve prolapse) and allergies among others. When the body lacks magnesium, it has difficulties in using proteins, enzymes and some antioxidants like vitamin C and vitamin E.

Magnesium is also important for detoxification and methylation purposes so, with our increasingly toxic environment, we absolutely need to increase our magnesium intake. Stress also has the property of increasing our magnesium requirements. The use of pesticides and herbicides decreases the quality of the soil, which leads to a lack of essential minerals.

Several other supplements may be of interest to combat athletes such as protein, creatine, amino acids (EAA), etc. But the inevitable ones are without a doubt the multivitamin, minerals, omega-3s, and magnesium."

CHAPTER 11

KIDS BJJ DEVELOPMENT

Why is it harder to be bilingual in adulthood than during our childhood? Because the brain areas that intervene are not the same according to age. Studies have found that in early bilingual children, the treatment of both languages was concentrated in a single area (left frontal lobe), whereas in the later, each language was treated in two distinct areas, resulting from loss of plasticity of the main area. This would explain the difficulties of 'late' adults in all areas, including traditional martial arts. Even if your kids do not seem to have the martial or combative spirit, enroll them in a martial art school and my choice is obvious, #brazilianjiujitsu in order to have the basics of self-defense" as an automatism " as they do with their multiplication table.

"One of the best things you can give to your kids is a skill. "

I have during my strength coach career come across many amazing young athletes. They had great talent. But unfortunately, there is a rampant problem in kids' athletic development, and it starts right at home. Early specific development is an ongoing issue that I come across a lot. I'm a big believer that for young kids, you need to immerse them in many sports. Each one of them brings different strengths, coordination, team or individual play, tactics, new movement patterns, etc. Early sports specialization is the worst thing you can do to them. Learning new movement skills at a young age is imperative. Focus on developing fundamental skills at an early age. They will have a larger base to grow from. I couldn't care less of what your kids' coach says, all they want is to capitalize on your kids "early talent" to better their organization or team by getting more kids in to increase their revenue. If a coach is telling you that your son or daughter needs to specialize instead of developing, he may be more concerned with chasing a trophy to put in his man cave to show off to or for his school achievements than your son/daughter's well being.

"Every child needs to learn how to swim, ride and fight" -Helio Gracie

In fact, a new study by the University of Wisconsin School of Medicine and Public Health which included over 1,500 high school athletes found that athletes who specialized in one sport were twice as likely to report a lower extremity injury as compared to those who played multiple sports. It was also found that 60% of athletes that specialized in one sport sustained a new lower extremity injury

" 88% of college athletes participated in more than one sport as a child."
-Dr. Greg Schaible

With that being said, we've been advocating sports and health as a priority since my kids were very young. We asked them what they would like to do. They have done and still do dance, soccer, tae kwon do, and now, all they want to do is Brazilian Jiu-Jitsu. I still want them to do other sports, but at least, I can rest thinking that at least, they know how to defend themselves.

"Giving your kids skills is better than giving them one thousand pieces of gold"
–Chinese proverb

After 12-14 years old, this is actually the best time to start looking at what they like, because at that age, most of their coordination has been acquired and you can also start seeing what they are driven to and what talent they seem to have.

There is always the age-old myth about how strength training can stunt growth but in fact, there is no scientific evidence to this myth. What is supported by scientific evidence and research is that properly designed and supervised resistance training programs have numerous benefits for kids, including; increasing strength and bone strength index, decreasing fracture risk and rates of sports-related injury, growing self-esteem and interest in fitness. Dr. Avery Faigenbaum of the University of Massachusetts states that concerns about weight lifting and the possible growth stunt of children and adolescents are outdated and misleading. He suggests that eating a healthy diet and exercising regularly allow you to achieve your maximal height, with inactive, unhealthy eaters more likely to have stunted growth.

The concerns come from doctors who believed that weight lifting can have a negative impact on growth plates steaming from research that most injuries and fractures at a young age involve growth plates. The thing is that lifting too heavy with faulty technique will always, young or old, cause some structural issues on the body. Growth plates are most susceptible to injuries because they are softer at a young age compared to the older population, which is why supervision is a must when they start weight lifting.

The next question is; at what age should they start strength training? My approach doesn't change much when it comes to kids. Rehab and injury prevention first is primordial. Now, at a young age, there is not much rehab to do compared to adults with years of structural issues and injuries, unless there is some kind of issues to deal with. Again, what I see most are postural concerns. It could be from the knees buckling in and upper back slouching, the result of structural issues and faulty neuromuscular patterns. Although I always recommend a personalized approach, here are some useful tips; (Side note; those tips are good for everyone)

Tip #1 Volume
They don't have to go all out at the gym and in fact, they shouldn't. Start with the minimum and build from there. The myth of stunt growth also comes from gymnasts. Look at their heights; they are often shorter than the average girls. The amount of training they go through, especially if they compete is often ridiculous. A minimum of 3 hours a day, for many years. I've often seen some of these young girls have a growth spurt once they retire around the age of 16-18 years old.

They should strength train no more than twice a week, focusing on basic strength.

Tip #2 Build a strong and solid base
Like in sports, I focus on acquiring skills. After a few weeks of fixing structural issues, we can start working on strength. 2-3 exercises like bench press or push-ups, pull-ups or TRX rows, deadlifts and/or squats. Focus on full range of movements, ALWAYS! Once you start with a bad habit or decreased range of movements, it creates faulty joint patterns. Here comes trouble.

Tip #3 Quality over quantity
Never sacrifice the quality of a movement for more weight, especially at a young age.

Tip #4 The kaisen method
If there is one method that is very effective with the younger population is the kaisen method, where you do small increments of weight. Small could be as low as 1 pound per workout. Small improvements are still improvements and over time, they cumulate huge progress.

Tip #5 Health

Do it with a purpose. Lifting weights is not only about getting stronger, it helps body composition, concentration, it brings better eating habits, helps gain lean and metabolically active muscle, but on top of it all, it is for overall health and boosts overall confidence. Kids not to get off their butt and stay active. They get less of it in school, they get home and go straight on Fortnite or any other games on their phone or console. They don't get to socialize as much as we did outside of school and enjoy what a kid's life should be. My mom kicked me out of the house to go play with my friends. To tell you the truth, she really didn't have to. I remember her trying to come and get me because I was everywhere, and stayed until the sun came down or later.

If done correctly, you can even start them as young as 8 years old. The main idea is to put an emphasis on movement. Use bodyweight exercises to start with and make it fun. As they master the correct movement.

Here is how a sample workout would look like. 3 sets of 10-15 reps on each exercise with rest periods of 60 to 90 seconds between each.

8-12 years old

Push-ups
Lunges
Pullups bar holds (up to 10 seconds)
Deadlifts

Very basic moves. The goal is to teach the movements without loading at first. Full range of motion and slow. The most common mistake I see with parents and especially coaches is to OVERTEACH a movement.. They don't have to get it on the first try. The worst case I see (often) is coaches who tell their kids for deadlift to squeeze the butt, contract the core, lookup, shoulders back, breath, knees in line with the feet, while they did not even grab the bar yet.

I do the opposite, I show them once by explaining the main idea. Point out 2 or three important things and that's it. I tell them to grab the bar and go. Then I fix the main issues one by one, every subsequent set. I never failed to teach basic moves under 3 sets. If this simple method can't be applied, the exercise is probably too complicated for them. Revise and change accordingly.

Once a solid base is established, more complex moves can be included.

Generally, like the soul purpose of this book, making the program while keeping in mind the specificity of the sport is the next logical step.

For kids, my advice would be to work on the core and making sure that the knees are healthy. Exercises such as split squats, step-ups, and lunges are best for developing knee stability and integrity. Next would be the posterior chain as it is one of the most important aspects of an athlete's strength, power and explosiveness.

As you can see, these tips are somewhat similar to beginners. One way or another, the basics should never stay very far from your programs. A full-grown adult could use the basic 8-12 years old program mentioned earlier and get crazy results from it. In fact, the kid should find it way easier than us. The fact that our nervous system is a lot more developed and that adults have in general more muscle mass than they do are some of the reasons why basics can seem easy for them and may, in many cases, be harder for us adults.

Control the basics, never stay far from it. The benefits are plenty.

CHAPTER 12

SPECIALISATION

There are many ways to build strength for sports, but there might be special exercises you can use to up the game, which is what I call the unfair advantage. They can up your cardio, your grips strength, overall strength, core functions, maybe all at once! The only downside is that they are not what you see in your regular gyms. You might have to go into those underground gyms were you see the most incredible feats of strength by the regulars. You could also buy most of these pieces of equipment and call them your own. It's a small investment for the return you would get

Rogue globe, balls, and Dogbone

Those can be very efficient when trying to increase grip strength. The Globe is more like holding the head of someone which is great for the grappling standing head clinch.

The dog bone could be grabbed in many ways like mixed grip (picture), pronated or supinated grip or the toughest way would be to hold it at each extremity. The ball-shaped extremities make it impossible to hold it so you'll have to take on an overhand grip which involves not only gripping strength but wrist flexion, a very important aspect of grappling and holding strength. As for the small balls, those are best for finger strength. All of these special pieces can be hooked up to pulleys so they could replace the original lat-pulldown attachments for those unable to do pull ups. I also use them to pull sleds, prowlers or even my jeep.

Bongo board and swiss ball

A method I enjoy is to fire up the nervous system at the same time as I warm up the body. We use the Swiss ball and the bongo board to simulate the flow of movement, the feeling of surfing we get from the flow rolls. Wakes you up and gets you ready to go!

The Bongo Board is an advanced type of balance training device. The board stands on a cylindrical roller so it offers another degree of instability. It`s often used by skiers, snowboarders, skaters, surfers, golfers, basketball and football players and others for effective training.

Bongo Boards are designed mainly for advanced users but even beginners will experience a lot of fun.

Wrist roller

Great tool for grip endurance and forearms. The goal is to roll the weight that is attached all the way up by only using the forearms.

Chains and bands.

Let's say you are at the bottom, and they are trying to get a cross-side for example. In training, you can benchpress 180 lbs, the weight of average male. They grab your neck and gi, and try to gain position and pull, the weight suddenly becomes 250 lbs trying to crash down on you. For the strength challenged, no way will you be able to hold them. Here's one tip to improve strength.

Enter accommodating resistance

During a lift, not all joint angles require the same amount of force. For example, you can top ¼ squat 300 pounds but can only do a full squat with 200lbs. The use of chains and bands helps increase the amount of force applied to accommodate the descending strength curve, like the end range of benchpress or squats for example. In BJJ, strength/speed is the mother of qualities required. One of the benefits of bands has to do with the force-velocity curve. "The more velocity developed, the less force needed to move the object." If you lift a weight with great speed, the less force is needed to complete the lift. Increasing strength is a must. Strength is the mother of all qualities.

We also must look at deceleration! Ever got crushed by someone heavier? Slowing them down, that's called deceleration. Remember our 180lbs strong opponent? Training for strength gives you this advantage. For the well-trained individual, you can eccentrically lower a weight of 130 to 140% of your max benchpress weight. So fighting a heavier or stronger opponent might get easier if well trained and prepared. Bands/chains would be great tools to improve speed/strength and strength/speed, add them to your arsenal.

The difference between chains and bands is that bands increase the resistance at the top of the movement exponentially. Chains increase incrementally and slowly. I would use chains for speed/strength and chains for power but still could have an impact on speed and explosiveness.

Depending on the chains, some links are between 0.5 to 1 one pound each. If used for example the Bench Press, it would come out as a 7 to 14 pounds difference from the bottom to the top position.

Chains are used to increase power and explosiveness. It adds weight incrementally when your strength curve is at its strongest and the joint is extended, like in a bench press or a squat. This is called the ascending strength curve, it adds more weight when you are at your strongest.

One chain (top) is useless in my opinion. Using a few chains is best (bottom). The aim is to have a 30 to 50-pound difference between the bottom and the top position of the lift, or even heavier for the squats.

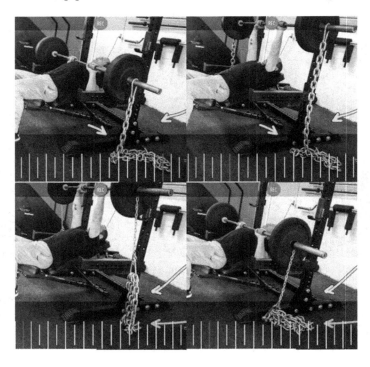

Sit fit

With all the possible ways to injure the knee and ankles in jiujitsu and grappling, rehabbing and injury prevention is never to be neglected. Sissel's SIT FIT primary use is to help alleviate lower back tension while working and sitting all day. It is basically a cushion filled with air that you sit on and makes your hips constantly move which stimulates blood flow to the lower extremities and alleviates pressure on the lower spine. Although it is mostly designed for lower back issues, it can also help the ankles. You can simply stand on one foot or do one of my favorite exercises for lower extremities, the split squats. Put the front foot on top of the sit fit and execute the movement. For added difficulty, no shoes required.

Buffalo bar

The only problem with the regular barbell bench press is that you can't really vary grip positions besides increasing the width of where you grab the bar. This specialty barbell increases the variety of grips and can be of great help when wrist problems are lurking. There is no best way to grab a dumbbell. Lifters usually fall between the neutral (like holding a hammer) and semi supinated grip (hand at 45°). This is great with a Dumbell but when using the benchpress, being able to use the same grip can help bring on more variety and power.

Rogue Mas wrestling board

A mix of full-body strength training, friendly competition, and hand-to-hand combat, MAS wrestling has grown from a small regional tradition in northern Russia to an event seen at Strongman competitions and open tournaments across the globe.

MAS wrestling is a two-man tug of war using a wooden stick. Sitting on the floor, competitors facing each other, feet pressed against the footboard divider in-between them. When the match starts, both competitors have a grip on the stick (or the Mas as they call it). The main goal is to break the grip of your opponent or to throw your opponent over the divider.

But I always like to spice things up. I use a Gi and the winner is the one who ends up with the full Gi on his side.

Rogue grip strength trainer

The Rogue Grip Trainer is designed with a slide mechanism consisting of two parallel steel prongs. You pull on the steel rods which could be attached to elastics or weights hanging by a strap, or both for added pleasure. Great tool for developing superior, lasting grip strength.

Bandbell bamboo bar (earthquake)

The earthquake bar is great for conducting and targeting kinetic energy to the shoulders, elbows, biceps and lower back to heal and strengthen stabilizing muscles and allow for healthy joint function. Shoulder strength is of the utmost importance in BJJ and this is the greatest tool.

Abs and core

The Turkish get-up

For the Turkish, core strength is the main player. Although it is a matter of proper positioning, you'll need strength since no Turkish in BJJ is the same. You basically do it against a force trying to bring you back down, unless he messed up along the way and has no clue about posting and limb positioning. Streetwise, the technical get up (top pictures), which is part of the Turkish, is a way of fending off or keeping the opponent at a distance since one arm stays in front. When finishing a sweep like the Ashi Garami, using the technical get up helps controlling one leg while keeping the ability to pass safely.

You could practice the Turkish with a barbell or a dumbbell as shown in the middle pictures where the barbell requires a lot more stability from the wrist and shoulder. Lying down while holding the weight as perpendicular as possible to the floor, crunch up and post on your elbow, continue the push-off on to your hand to bring the leg back and post on your knee. Get up by pushing the weight towards the ceiling. Reverse the steps to go back down.

For #BJJ, you don't have to get up, unless it's after a sweep to get points. Often, to get out of cross-side or mount, you might have to use the first portion of the Turkish, which is the initial push-off. Use a band to add a little more challenge. As the weight is constant with a barbell or dumbbell, the resistance increases exponentially with a band as you go up as shown in the lower right picture.

Side plank

I have seen many low back issues in my career and one of the most neglected muscles of the core is the quadratus lumborum, a muscle of the posterior abdominal wall. It is the deepest abdominal muscle and commonly referred to as a back muscle. It is irregular and quadrilateral in shape. It is one of the prime movers of lateral flexion of the spine, bending sideways.

You are lying on your side with your elbow and feet touching the floor while holding your hips up. You can do it for time or do 3 sets of 10 reps on each side.

Leg raises

5 levels of hanging raise
1. knee raise
2. leg raise
3. leg raise to reverse crunch
4. skin the cat (full leg raise to inverted, healthy and strong shoulders required)
5. Load shifting knee raise to slow eccentric straight leg

And that's only 10% of the basic variations and what we can do with these rings.

Final Oss

There is a saying that goes 'It's better to be in the arena, getting stomped by the bull, than to be up in the stands or out in the parking lot.' If there is one thing you can learn from this book is that all around performance not only depends on one workout, or how many drills you do in a month. Maximizing performance is multifactorial. It's as if you want to create the perfect storm.

Nutrition, strength and conditioning, drills, rolls, rest, nutrition, rest and repeat. I know, I wrote nutrition and rest twice. Some elements need more attention than others since they can also tell you if you are messing up or not. The body has a way to send you signs as symptoms, which is why I included the habits chapter.

I hope you find this book helpful and that it gives you more years on the mats. Roll strong(er) and enjoy the ride!

MACRO NUTRIENT TABLE

Proteins	carbs	Fats
Serving size: 3-6 oz. cooked, or as indicated. Meat, poultry, and fish should be grilled, baked or roasted; fish can also be poached. Keep cheese intake low due to saturated fat (1 serving = approximately 150 calories) Eggs, 2 whole, or 3 egg whites plus 1 whole egg Poultry: chicken or Cornish hen (breast only), turkey Leg of lamb, lean roast Fish, shellfish, 3 oz. fresh or 3/4 cup canned in water Beef, very lean, wild game (ostrich, bison, wild boar, rabbit, etc)	**Lower glycemic index carbs, Serving size: 1/2 cup - servings unlimited Fresh juices made from these are allowed (1 serving = approximately 10-25 calories)** Artichokes Bean sprouts, Brussels sprouts Celery, Dill pickles, Greens: bok choy, escarole, Swiss chard, kale, collard greens, spinach, dandelion, mustard, or beet greens, Okra, Sea vegetables (kelp, etc.), Tomatoes or mixed vegetable juice, Asparagus, Bell or other peppers, Cabbage (all types), Chives, onion, leeks, garlic, Eggplant, Lettuce/Mixed greens: romaine, red and green leaf, endive, spinach, arugula, radicchio, watercress, chicory, Radishes Snow peas, Water chestnuts, 5 whole, Bamboo shoots, Broccoli, Broccoflower, Cauliflower Cucumber,, Green Beans Mushrooms, Salsa (sugar free) Sprouts, Zucchini, yellow, summer, or spaghetti squash **Higher Glycemic index carbs, Serving size: 1/2 cup, or as indicated (1 serving = approximately 45 calories)** Beets, winter squash, such as acorn or butternut squash, Yukon Gold Potato, 1/2 medium, Carrots, 1/2 cup cooked or 2 medium raw or 12 baby carrots, Sweet Potatoes or yams, 1/2 medium baked **Fruits Serving size as indicated (1 serving = approximately 80 calories)** Apple, 1 medium, Cantaloupe, 1/2 medium, Grapefruit, 1 whole, Mango, 1/2 medium, Peaches, 2 small Tangerines, 2 small, Apricots, 3 medium, Cherries, 15, Grapes, 15, Nectarines, 2 small, Pear, 1 medium, **Berries: blackberries & blueberries, 1 cup; raspberries & strawberries, 1 1/2 cups**, Fresh figs, 2, Honeydew melon, 1/4 small, Orange, 1 large Plums, 2 small	**Nuts and seeds Serving size as indicated (1 serving = approximately 100 calories)** Almonds or hazelnuts, 10-12 whole nuts, Pistachios, sunflower, pumpkin, or sesame seeds, 2 tbsp. Oils Walnut or pecan halves, 7-8 Nut butter, 1 tbsp. made from above nuts Peanuts, 18 nuts or 2 tbsp. **Oils Serving size: 1 tsp. or as indicated Otis should be cold-pressed (1 serving = approximately 40 calories)** Avocado, 1/8 Extra virgin olive oil (preferable) & canola oil for cooking, Flaxseed oil (refrigerate), Mayonnaise (from canola oil), Walnut oil Olives, 8-10 medium

Wake up Time:	
Morning meal Time:	
Snack Time:	
Mid day meal Time:	
Snack Time:	
Evening meal Time:	
Snack Time:	
Water intake	
Activity Type duration	
Relaxation	

Phase 1

Day1 white belt

	exercise	Sets/reps	Tempo	rest	W1		W2		W3		W4	
A 1	Flat db press	3x6-8 1x10	4010	75s	w	r	w	r	w	r	w	r
A 2	neutral gr. pulldown	3x6-8 1x10	4010	75s	w	r	w	r	w	r	w	r
B 1	ext. rot. On knee	3x 10-12	4010	30s	w	r	w	r	w	r	w	r
B 2	Row collar bone	3x 12-15	4010	60s	w	r	w	r	w	r	w	r
C 1	Low.Inc. lying ext.	3x6-8 1x10	4010	75s	w	r	w	r	w	r	w	r
C 2	45' inc. db curl neutral grip	3x6-8 1x10	4010	75s	w	r	w	r	w	r	w	r

Day2 white belt

	exercise	Sets/reps	Tempo	rest	W1		W2		W3		W4	
A 1	DB split squat FF elevated	3x6-8 1x10	4010	75s	w	r	w	r	w	r	w	r
A 2	lying leg curl	3x6-8 1x10	4010	75s	w	r	w	r	w	r	w	r
B 1	mixed grip rom. deadlift	3x 8-10	4010	30s	w	r	w	r	w	r	w	r
B 2	Db step up	3x 12-15	4010	60s	w	r	w	r	w	r	w	r
C 1	st calf raise one leg	3x 10-12	4010	75s	w	r	w	r	w	r	w	r
C 2	QL lift	3x 8-10	4010	75s	w	r	w	r	w	r	w	r

Day 1 blue belt

	exercise	Sets/reps	Tempo	rest	W1		W2		W3		W4	
A1	flat db press fat grips	3x6-8 1x10	4010	75s	w	r	w	r	w	r	w	r
A2	neutral grip pullups	3x6-8 1x10	4010	75s	w	r	w	r	w	r	w	r
B1	seat. Ext. rot. On knee fat gr.	3x 6-8	4010	30s	w	r	w	r	w	r	w	r
B2	row to forehead w/ rope	3x 10-12	4010	60s	w	r	w	r	w	r	w	r
C1	flat Lying Ext. DB fat gr.	3x6-8 1x10	4010	75s	w	r	w	r	w	r	w	r
C2	30° incl. zottman curl	3x6-8 1x10	4010	75s	w	r	w	r	w	r	w	r

Day2 Blue Belt

	exercise	Sets/reps	Tempo	rest	W1		W2		W3		W4	
A1	DB split squats	3x6-8 1x10	4010	75s	w	r	w	r	w	r	w	r
A2	Lying leg curl plantar flex.	3x6-8 1x10	4010	75s	w	r	w	r	w	r	w	r
B1	rom. Deadlift pron. Gr.	3x 8-10	4010	30s	w	r	w	r	w	r	w	r
B2	cyclist squats	3x 12-15	4010	60s	w	r	w	r	w	r	w	r
C1	St. calf raise one legged	3x 10-12	4010	75s	w	r	w	r	w	r	w	r
C2	hang. Knee to chest (garhammer)	3x6-8 or max	4010	75s	w	r	w	r	w	r	w	r

Day 1 Purple belt

	exercise	Sets/reps	Tempo	rest	W1		W2		W3		W4	
A 1	close pron. pullups	3x6-8 1x10	4010	75s	w	r	w	r	w	r	w	r
A 2	barbell split squats	3x6-8 1x10	4010	75s	w	r	w	r	w	r	w	r
B 1	seat. Row to neck rope	3x6-8 1x10	4010	75s	w	r	w	r	w	r	w	r
B 2	barbell front squats	3x6-8 1x10	4010	75s	w	r	w	r	w	r	w	r
C 1	Flat db lying ext. fat grip	3x 8-10	4010	60s	w	r	w	r	w	r	w	r
C 2	incl. db curl 30° pron. Grip fat grips	3x 8-10	4010	60s	w	r	w	r	w	r	w	r

Day2 purple belt

	exercise	Sets/reps	Tempo	rest	W1		W2		W3		W4	
A 1	BB snatch gr. deadlift	3x6-8 1x10	4010	75s	w	r	w	r	w	r	w	r
A 2	BB 20° incl close gr. press	3x6-8 1x10	4010	75s	w	r	w	r	w	r	w	r
B 1	Acc. Lying Leg curl	3x6-8 1x10	4010	75s	w	r	w	r	w	r	w	r
B 2	St. BB press shoulder width	3x6-8 1x10	4010	75s	w	r	w	r	w	r	w	r
C 1	Hanging Toes to bar	3x 8-10	4010	60s	w	r	w	r	w	r	w	r
C 2	Neck bridges Swiss ball	3x 8-10	4010	60s	w	r	w	r	w	r	w	r

Phase 2

White belt day 1
Chest and back

	exercise	Sets/reps	Tempo	rest	W1		W2		W3		W4	
A1	incl. BB bench 30° shoulder width	(8,6,4) x2	3010	90s	w	r	w	r	w	r	w	r
A2	Eccentric pull ups	(8,6,4) x2	5010	90s	w	r	w	r	w	r	w	r
B1	St. db shoulder press Unilateral	3x 6-8	3020	30s	w	r	w	r	w	r	w	r
B2	one arm bent-over row	3x 6-8	3020	60s	w	r	w	r	w	r	w	r
C	mid pulley ext rot (elbow on hip)	3x 8-10	4010	75s	w	r	w	r	w	r	w	r

White belt day 2
Legs

	exercise	Sets/reps	Tempo	rest	W1		W2		W3		W4	
A1	DB squats heels elevated	(8,6,4) x2	3020	90s	w	r	w	r	w	r	w	r
A2	Lying leg curl ecc. Plantar conc. dorsi	(8,6,4) x2	3020	90s	w	r	w	r	w	r	w	r
B1	low pulley split squats	3x 6-8	4010	30s	w	r	w	r	w	r	w	r
B2	Romanian deadlift	3x 6-8	4010	60s	w	r	w	r	w	r	w	r
C	incl. hyper extension	3x 8-10	4010	75s	w	r	w	r	w	r	w	r

White belt day 3
Arms

	exercise	Sets/ reps	Tempo	rest	W1		W2		W3		W4	
A 1	Flat benchpress fat close grip press (triceps)	(8,6,4) x2	3010	90s	w	r	w	r	w	r	w	r
A 2	Standing barbell curl EZ bar	(8,6,4) x2	5010	90s	w	r	w	r	w	r	w	r
B 1	flat barbell lying extension EZ bar	3x 6-8	3020	30s	w	r	w	r	w	r	w	r
B 2	preacher curl 45° neutral grip	3x 6-8	3020	60s	w	r	w	r	w	r	w	r
C	standing mid pulley one arm row to neck	3x 8-10	4010	75s	w	r	w	r	w	r	w	r

Blue belt Day 1
Chest/back

	exercise	Sets/ reps	Tempo	rest	W1		W2		W3		W4	
A 1	Flat db press neutral fat grips	(8,6,4) x2	3020	90s	w	r	w	r	w	r	w	r
A 2	medium mixed grip pull ups	(8,6,4) x2	3020	90s	w	r	w	r	w	r	w	r
B 1	seated barbell front press unsupported	3x 6-8	4010	30s	w	r	w	r	w	r	w	r
B 2	bent-over barbell row supinated grip	3x 6-8	4010	60s	w	r	w	r	w	r	w	r
C	standing barbell cobra	3x 8-10	4010	75s	w	r	w	r	w	r	w	r

Blue belt day 2
Legs/abs

	exercise	Sets/reps	Tempo	rest	W1		W2		W3		W4	
A1	Barbell back squats	(8,6,4) x2	3020	90s	w	r	w	r	w	r	w	r
A2	lying leg curl accentuated, plantar flexed toes in	(8,6,4) x2	3020	90s	w	r	w	r	w	r	w	r
B1	DB walking lunges	3x 6-8	4010	30s	w	r	w	r	w	r	w	r
B2	Barbell seated good morning	3x 6-8	4010	60s	w	r	w	r	w	r	w	r
C	garhammer raise	3x 8-10	4010	75s	w	r	w	r	w	r	w	r

Blue belt day 3
Triceps/biceps/forearms

	exercise	Sets/reps	Tempo	rest	W1		W2		W3		W4	
A1	Incline benchpress fat grip shoulder width	(8,6,4) x2	3020	90s	w	r	w	r	w	r	w	r
A2	Scott bench 45° zottman curl	(8,6,4) x2	3020	90s	w	r	w	r	w	r	w	r
B1	Decline DB lying extension	3x 6-8	4010	30s	w	r	w	r	w	r	w	r
B2	incline swiss ball curl neutral grip	3x 6-8	4010	60s	w	r	w	r	w	r	w	r
C	pronated grip ez bar curl	3x 8-10	4010	75s	w	r	w	r	w	r	w	r

Purple belt Day 1
Chest/back/shoulders

	exercise	Sets/reps	Tempo	rest	W1		W2		W3		W4	
A1	Flat benchpress close grip low pins	(8,6,4) x2	3020	90s	w	r	w	r	w	r	w	r
A2	Side to side pullups (right and left counts for 2 reps)	(8,6,4) x2	3020	90s	w	r	w	r	w	r	w	r
B1	swiss ball incline db fly, supination to pronation	3x 6-8	3020	30s	w	r	w	r	w	r	w	r
B2	one arm bent-over row to neck	3x 6-8	3020	60s	w	r	w	r	w	r	w	r
C	incline 30° powell raise pronated grip	3x 8-10	4010	75s	w	r	w	r	w	r	w	r

Purple belt day 2
Lower body/abs

	exercise	Sets/reps	Tempo	rest	W1		W2		W3		W4	
A1	Barbell front squats	(8,6,4) x2	3020	90s	w	r	w	r	w	r	w	r
A2	lying leg curl plantar flexed	(8,6,4) x2	3020	90s	w	r	w	r	w	r	w	r
B1	Barbell lunges	3x 6-8	4010	30s	w	r	w	r	w	r	w	r
B2	Glute ham raise	3x 6-8	4010	60s	w	r	w	r	w	r	w	r
C	Russian flag load shifting	3x 8-10	4010	75s	w	r	w	r	w	r	w	r

Purple belt day 3
Triceps/biceps/forearms

	exercise	Sets/reps	Tempo	rest	W1		W2		W3		W4	
A1	triceps dips	(8,6,4) x2	3020	90s	w	r	w	r	w	r	w	r
A2	one arm scott bench neutral grip curs	(8,6,4) x2	3020	90s	w	r	w	r	w	r	w	r
B1	low pulley rope lying extension neutral to supination	3x 6-8	4010	30s	w	r	w	r	w	r	w	r
B2	incline DB 30° supinated grip curls	3x 6-8	4010	60s	w	r	w	r	w	r	w	r
C	standing behind back standing wrist curls	3x 8-10	4010	75s	w	r	w	r	w	r	w	r

Phase 3 Contrast training

White belt Day 1

	exercise	Sets/reps	Tempo	rest	W1		W2		W3		W4	
A1	close grip tricep benchpress	4x 3-5	3020	30s	w	r	w	r	w	r	w	r
A2	medicine ball floor throws	4x 6-8	10X0	60s	w	r	w	r	w	r	w	r
A3	Pull ups neutral grip	4x 3-5	4010	30s	w	r	w	r	w	r	w	r
A4	med ball slam down	4x 6-8	10X0	120 s	w	r	w	r	w	r	w	r
B	Seated row to neck one arm pronated grip	3x 8-12	4010	75s	w	r	w	r	w	r	w	r
C1	Dips Feet forward	3x 8-12	4010	75s	w	r	w	r	w	r	w	r
C2	incline zottman curl	3x 8-12	4010	75s	w	r	w	r	w	r	w	r

White belt day 2

	exercise	Sets/ reps	Tempo	rest	W1		W2		W3		W4	
A 1	DB split squats	4x 3-5	3020	30s	w	r	w	r	w	r	w	r
A 2	Barbell step up (mid calf level)	4x 6-8	10X0	60s	w	r	w	r	w	r	w	r
A 3	Lying leg curl	4x 3-5	4010	30s	w	r	w	r	w	r	w	r
A 4	Pull through low pulley	4x 6-8	20X0	120 s	w	r	w	r	w	r	w	r
B 1	Db squats heels elevated	3x 8-12	4010	75s	w	r	w	r	w	r	w	r
B 2	unilateral lying or standing leg curl	3x 8-12	4010	75s	w	r	w	r	w	r	w	r

phase 3
Blue belt
Day 1

Chest/back

	exercise	Sets/ reps	Tempo	rest	W1		W2		W3		W4	
A 1	incline benchpress 30°	4x 3-5	3020	30s	w	r	w	r	w	r	w	r
A 2	medicine ball chest throws on wall	4x 6-8	10X0	60s	w	r	w	r	w	r	w	r
A 3	fat grip pull ups shoulder width	4x 3-5	4010	30s	w	r	w	r	w	r	w	r
A 4	med ball or heavy ball slam down	4x 6-8	10X0	120 s	w	r	w	r	w	r	w	r
B 1	flat db press	3x 8-12	4010	75s	w	r	w	r	w	r	w	r
B 2	seated row attach a gi to the pulley, lapel grip	3x 8-12	4010	75s	w	r	w	r	w	r	w	r

Blue belt
Day2
Lower body

	exercise	Sets/ reps	Tempo	rest	W1		W2		W3		W4	
A 1	Barbell back squats	4x 3-5	3020	30s	w	r	w	r	w	r	w	r
A 2	prowler sprints 10sec. (or penta jumps)	4x 6-8	10X0	60s	w	r	w	r	w	r	w	r
A 3	Lying leg curl	4x 3-5	10X0	30s	w	r	w	r	w	r	w	r
A 4	kettlebell swing	4x 6-8	10X0	120 s	w	r	w	r	w	r	w	r
B 1	leg press 45°	3x 8-12	4010	75s	w	r	w	r	w	r	w	r
B 2	Romanian deadlift (stiff legged)	3x 8-12	4010	75s	w	r	w	r	w	r	w	r

Blue belt
Day 3
Triceps/biceps

	exercise	Sets/ reps	Tempo	rest	W1		W2		W3		W4	
A 1	DB close grip tricep press flat	4x 3-5	3020	30s	w	r	w	r	w	r	w	r
A 2	Clapping push ups	4x 6-8	10X0	60s	w	r	w	r	w	r	w	r
A 3	incline db curl 45°	4x 3-5	4010	30s	w	r	w	r	w	r	w	r
A 4	heavy ball toss	4x 6-8	10X0	120s	w	r	w	r	w	r	w	r
B 1	scott bench 45° zottman curl	3x 8-12	4010	75s	w	r	w	r	w	r	w	r
B 2	high pulley towel tricep pushdown	3x 8-12	4010	75s	w	r	w	r	w	r	w	r

Phase 3
Purple belt
Day1

Chest/back

	exercise	Sets/reps	Tempo	rest	W1		W2		W3		W4	
A1	incline db press 30°	4x 3-5	3020	30s	w	r	w	r	w	r	w	r
A2	medicine ball floor throws	4x 6-8	10X0	60s	w	r	w	r	w	r	w	r
A3	Gi pullups	4x 3-5	4010	30s	w	r	w	r	w	r	w	r
A4	med ball slam down	4x 6-8	4010	120 s	w	r	w	r	w	r	w	r
B1	flat benchpress low pins	3x 8-12	4010	75s	w	r	w	r	w	r	w	r
B2	bent-over barbell row	3x 8-12	4010	75s	w	r	w	r	w	r	w	r

Purple belt
Day2

Lower body

	exercise	Sets/reps	Tempo	rest	W1		W2		W3		W4	
A1	barbell front squats	4x 3-5	3020	30s	w	r	w	r	w	r	w	r
A2	prowler sprints 10sec (penta jump)	4x 6-8	10X0	60s	w	r	w	r	w	r	w	r
A3	barbell deadlift	4x 3-5	4010	30s	w	r	w	r	w	r	w	r
A4	kettlebell swings	4x 6-8	10X0	120 s	w	r	w	r	w	r	w	r
B1	barbell split squats	3x 8-12	4010	75s	w	r	w	r	w	r	w	r
B2	barbell good morning	3x 8-12	4010	75s	w	r	w	r	w	r	w	r

Purple belt
Day 3

Triceps/biceps

	exercise	Sets/reps	Tempo	rest	W1		W2		W3		W4	
A1	Dips	4x 3-5	3020	30s	w	r	w	r	w	r	w	r
A2	deficit push ups	4x 6-8	10X0	60s	w	r	w	r	w	r	w	r
A3	supinated grip chin ups	4x 3-5	4010	30s	w	r	w	r	w	r	w	r
A4	Gi prowler or sled rows	4x 6-8	4010	120 s	w	r	w	r	w	r	w	r
B1	triceps frenchpress low pulley	3x 8-12	4010	75s	w	r	w	r	w	r	w	r
B2	pronated grip barbell curls	3x 8-12	4010	75s	w	r	w	r	w	r	w	r

Brown belt
Day 1

	exercise	Sets/reps	Tempo	rest	W1		W2		W3		W4	
A1	Incline db press 30°	4/6-8	3010	30s	w	r	w	r	w	r	w	r
A2	Seated row to neck with rope	4/6-8	3010	30s	w	r	w	r	w	r	w	r
B1	Flat benchpress	5/2-4	3010	120s	w	r	w	r	w	r	w	r
B2	Neutral grip pullups	5/2-4	3010	120s	w	r	w	r	w	r	w	r
C1	Low incline db fly (10-20°)	6/6-8	4010	30s	w	r	w	r	w	r	w	r
C2	One arm bent-over row	6/6-8	4010	30s	w	r	w	r	w	r	w	r

Brown belt
Day 2

	exercise	Sets/reps	Tempo	rest	W1		W2		W3		W4	
A1	DB split squats	4/6-8	3010	30s	w	r	w	r	w	r	w	r
A2	Romanian deadlift	4/6-8	3010	30s	w	r	w	r	w	r	w	r
B1	Barbell back squats	5/2-4	3010	120s	w	r	w	r	w	r	w	r
B2	Lying leg curl	5/2-4	3010	120s	w	r	w	r	w	r	w	r
C1	hyperextension	6/6-8	4010	30s	w	r	w	r	w	r	w	r
C2	Standing calf raise	6/6-8	4010	30s	w	r	w	r	w	r	w	r

Brown belt
Day 3

	exercise	Sets/reps	Tempo	rest	W1		W2		W3		W4	
A1	Barbell lying extension	4/6-8	3010	30s	w	r	w	r	w	r	w	r
A2	Pronated grip medium ez bar curl	4/6-8	3010	30s	w	r	w	r	w	r	w	r
B1	Close grip triceps barbell benchpress	5/2-4	3010	120s	w	r	w	r	w	r	w	r
B2	Standing barbell curl	5/2-4	3010	120s	w	r	w	r	w	r	w	r
C1	Low pulley frenchpress	6/6-8	4010	30s	w	r	w	r	w	r	w	r
C2	Scott bench 45° dn neutral grip	6/6-8	4010	30s	w	r	w	r	w	r	w	r

Black Belt
Day 1

	Exercise/% of 1rm	Sets/ week	reps	Tempo	rest	W1		W2		W3		W4	
A	benchpress	3 sets		3010	180	w	r	w	r	w	r	w	r
W1	65,75,85% (last 3 sets)		5			w	r	w	r	w	r	w	r
W2	70,80,90%		3			w	r	w	r	w	r	w	r
W3	75,85,95%		5,3,1			w	r	w	r	w	r	w	r
W4	40,50,60%		5			w	r	w	r	w	r	w	r
B	Standing shoulder press	5	8-10	3010	90s	w	r	w	r	w	r	w	r
C	Bent-over barbell row	5	8-10	3010	90s	w	r	w	r	w	r	w	r

Black Belt
Day 2

	Exercise/% of 1rm	Sets/ week	reps	Tempo	rest	W1		W2		W3		W4	
A	Barbell deadlift	3 sets		3010	180	w	r	w	r	w	r	w	r
W1	65,75,85% (last 3 sets)		5			w	r	w	r	w	r	w	r
W2	70,80,90%		3			w	r	w	r	w	r	w	r
W3	75,85,95%		5,3,1			w	r	w	r	w	r	w	r
W4	40,50,60%		5			w	r	w	r	w	r	w	r
B	Lying leg curl unilateral	5	8-10	3010	90s	w	r	w	r	w	r	w	r
C	Hanging leg raise	5	8-10	3010	90s	w	r	w	r	w	r	w	r

Black Belt
Day 3

		Exercise/% of 1rm	Sets/ week	reps	Tempo	rest	W1		W2		W3		W4	
A		Pull ups	3 sets		3010	180	w	r	w	r	w	r	w	r
W 1		65,75,85% (last 3 sets)		5			w	r	w	r	w	r	w	r
W 2		70,80,90%		3			w	r	w	r	w	r	w	r
W 3		75,85,95%		5,3,1			w	r	w	r	w	r	w	r
W 4		40,50,60%		5			w	r	w	r	w	r	w	r
B		Standing barbell press	5	8-10	3010	90s	w	r	w	r	w	r	w	r
C		Seated ext rotation on knee	5	8-10	3010	90s	w	r	w	r	w	r	w	r

Black Belt
Day 4

		Exercise/% of 1rm	Sets/ week	reps	Tempo	rest	W1		W2		W3		W4	
A		Back squats	3 sets		3010	180	w	r	w	r	w	r	w	r
W 1		65,75,85% (last 3 sets)		5			w	r	w	r	w	r	w	r
W 2		70,80,90%		3			w	r	w	r	w	r	w	r
W 3		75,85,95%		5,3,1			w	r	w	r	w	r	w	r
W 4		40,50,60%		5			w	r	w	r	w	r	w	r
B		DB split squats	5	8-10	3010	90s	w	r	w	r	w	r	w	r
C		Lying leg curl	5	8-10	3010	90s	w	r	w	r	w	r	w	r

Finishers

#1 Javorek style (to be performed at the end of a workout)

	exercise	Sets/reps	Tempo	rest	W1		W2		W3		W4	
A1	Barbell hang snatch	6 reps	10X0	0s	w	r	w	r	w	r	w	r
A2	Standing barbell squats	6 reps	30X0	0s	w	r	w	r	w	r	w	r
A3	Standing barbell press	6 reps	30X0	0s	w	r	w	r	w	r	w	r
A4	Snatch grip deadlift	6 reps	30X0	0s/120s	w	r	w	r	w	r	w	r

Method #1: Perform as many rounds as possible in 15 minutes, rest as needed
Method #2: 4 sets with 2 minutes rest after A4.
Always keep the same weight and never let go of the bar.

#2 Abs circuit

	exercise	Sets/reps	Tempo	rest	W1		W2		W3		W4	
A1	Floor bike (elbow/knee)	60sec		0s	w	r	w	r	w	r	w	r
A2	Mountain climber	60sec		0s	w	r	w	r	w	r	w	r
A3	Leg scissors	60sec		0s	w	r	w	r	w	r	w	r
A4	Plank	60sec		120s	w	r	w	r	w	r	w	r

4 sets with 2 minutes rest after A4.

#3 Row your boat (concept 2 rower)

	exercise	Sets/ reps	Tempo	rest	W1		W2		W3		W4	
A 1	Rower	500m X5		60s	w	r	w	r	w	r	w	r
	500 m intervals with 60 seconds rest between each.											

#4 Tabata style 4

	exercise	Sets/ reps	Tempo	rest	W1		W2		W3		W4	
A 1	DB/BB thrusters	20sec		10s	w	r	w	r	w	r	w	r
A 2	Rope battle	20sec		10s	w	r	w	r	w	r	w	r
A 3	Burpees	20sec		10s	w	r	w	r	w	r	w	r
	3 rounds of A1 to A3 take 2 minutes and repeat for 3 sets.											

---

[i] http://news.theopenmat.com/blog/2014/05/04/helen-maroulis-to-face-venezuelas-marcia-

andrades-at-beat-the-streets/

[ii] Sleep More, Lose Weight Getting Enough Snooze Time May Be The Best Diet Secret of All, By Mary Shomon,

[iii] de Baaij JH, Hoenderop JG, Bindels RJ. Magnesium in man: implications for health and disease. Physiol Rev. 2015 Jan;95(1):1-46. doi: 10.1152/physrev.00012.2014. Review. PubMed PMID: 25540137.

References:

1 http://www.webmd.com/a-to-z-guides/cortisol-14668 Effects of morning cortisol elevation on insulin secretion and glucose regulation in humans.Plat L, Byrne MM, Sturis J, Polonsky KS, Mockel J, Féry F, Van CauterE.Am J Physiol. 1996 Jan;270(1 Pt 1):E36-42.PMID:8772471[PubMed - indexed for MEDLINE]

2 Leidy HJ, Ortinau LC, Douglas SM, Hoertel HA. Beneficial effects of a higher-protein breakfast on the appetitive, hormonal, and neural signals controlling energy intake regulation in overweight/obese, "breakfast-skipping,"late-adolescent girls. Am J ClinNutr. 2013 Apr;97(4):677-88. doi:10.3945/ajcn.112.053116. Epub 2013 Feb 27. PubMed PMID: 23446906; PubMed Central PMCID: PMC3718776.

3 Pesta DH, Samuel VT. A high-protein diet for reducing body fat: mechanisms and possible caveats. NutrMetab (Lond). 2014 Nov 19;11(1):53. doi:10.1186/1743-7075-11-53. eCollection 2014. Review. PubMed PMID: 25489333; PubMed Central PMCID: PMC4258944.

4 van der Klaauw AA, Keogh JM, Henning E, Trowse VM, Dhillo WS, GhateiMA,Farooqi IS. High protein intake stimulates postprandial GLP1 and PYY release.Obesity (Silver Spring). 2013 Aug;21(8):1602-7. doi: 10.1002/oby.20154. Epub 2013 May 13. PubMed PMID: 23666746.

5 Cooper SB, Bandelow S, Nute ML, Morris JG, Nevill ME. Breakfast glycaemic index and cognitive function in adolescent school children. Br J Nutr. 2012 Jun;107(12):1823-32. doi: 10.1017/S0007114511005022. Epub 2011 Sep 29. PubMed PMID: 22017815.

6 Micha R, Rogers PJ, Nelson M. Glycaemic index and glycaemic load of breakfast predict cognitive function and mood in school children: a randomised controlled trial. Br J Nutr. 2011 Nov;106(10):1552-61. doi: 10.1017/S0007114511002303. Epub 2011 Jun 8. PubMed PMID: 21736777.

7 Mikael Nilsson, Marianne Stenberg, Anders H Frid, Jens J Holst, and Inger ME BjörckGlycemia and insulinemia in healthy subjects after lactose-equivalent meals of milk and other food proteins: the role of plasma amino acids and incretinsAm J ClinNutr November 2004 vol. 80 no. 5 1246-1253

8 Use of waist circumference to predict insulin resistance: retrospective studyBMJ 2005;330:1363 Paoli A, Marcolin G, Zonin F, Neri M, Sivieri A, Pacelli QF. Exercising fasting or fed to enhance fat loss? Influence of food intake on respiratory ratioand excess postexercise oxygen consumption after a bout of endurance training. Int J Sport NutrExercMetab. 2011 Feb;21(1):48-54. PubMed PMID: 21411835.

9 Lombardo M, Bellia A, Padua E, Annino G, Guglielmi V, D'Adamo M, IellamoF,Sbraccia P. Morning meal more efficient for fat loss in a 3-month lifestyle intervention. J Am CollNutr. 2014;33(3):198-205. doi:10.1080/07315724.2013.863169. Epub 2014 May 8. PubMed PMID: 24809437.

Leidy HJ, Ortinau LC, Douglas SM, Hoertel HA. Beneficial effects of a higher-protein breakfast on the appetitive, hormonal, and neural signalscontrolling energy intake regulation in overweight/obese, "breakfast-skipping,"late-adolescent girls. Am J ClinNutr. 2013 Apr;97(4):677-88. doi:10.3945/ajcn.112.053116. Epub 2013 Feb 27. PubMed PMID: 23446906; PubMed Central PMCID: PMC3718776.

[v] Manini TM. Energy expenditure and aging. Ageing Res Rev. 2010 Jan;9(1):1-11. doi: 10.1016/j.arr.2009.08.002. Epub 2009 Aug 19. Review. PubMed PMID: 19698803; PubMed Central PMCID: PMC2818133.
[vi] McMurray RG, Soares J, Caspersen CJ, McCurdy T. Examining variations of resting metabolic rate of adults: a public health perspective. Med Sci Sports Exerc. 2014 Jul;46(7):1352-8. doi: 10.1249/MSS.0000000000000232. Review. PubMed PMID: 24300125; PubMed Central PMCID: PMC4535334.
[vii] Harris Benedict formula for women and men. GottaSport.com. Retrieved on 2011-10-27.

[viii] Alexandra M. Johnstone, Sandra D. Murison, Jackie S. Duncan, Kellie A. Rance, and John R. Speakman, "Factors Influencing Variation in Basal Metabolic Rate Include Fat-Free Mass, Fat Mass, Age, and Circulating Thyroxine but Not Sex, Circulating Leptin, or Triiodothyronine," American Journal of Clinical Nutrition 82(5) (2005): 941– 48.

[ix] Lenard Lesser, Cara B. Ebbeling, Merrill Goozner, David Wypij, and David S. Ludwig, "Relationship Between Funding Source and Conclusion Among Nutrition-Related Scientific Articles," PLoS Medicine 4 (2007): e5.

[x] U.S. Department of Health and Human Services, "2008 Physical Activity Guidelines for Americans."

[xi] Satoru Kodama, Kazumi Saito, Shiro Tanaka, Miho Maki, Yoko Yachi, Mihoko Asumi, Ayumi Sugawara, et al., "Cardiorespiratory Fitness as a Quantitative Predictor of All-Cause Mortality and Cardiovascular Events in Healthy Men and Women: A Meta-analysis," Journal of the American Medical Association 301(19) (2009): 2024–35.

[xii] Hector A, Phillips SM. Protein Recommendations for Weight Loss in Elite Athletes: A Focus on Body Composition and Performance. Int J Sport Nutr Exerc Metab. 2017 Nov 28:1-26. doi: 10.1123/ijsnem.2017-0273. [Epub ahead of print] PubMed PMID: 29182451.

[xiii] Halton TL, Hu FB. The effects of high protein diets on thermogenesis, satiety and weight loss: a critical review. J Am Coll Nutr. 2004 Oct;23(5):373-85. Review. PubMed PMID: 15466943.

[xiv] Blom WA, Lluch A, Stafleu A, Vinoy S, Holst JJ, Schaafsma G, Hendriks HF. Effect of a high-protein breakfast on the postprandial ghrelin response. Am J Clin Nutr. 2006 Feb;83(2):211-20. PubMed PMID: 16469977.

[xv] Munger RG, Cerhan JR, Chiu BC. Prospective study of dietary protein intake and risk of hip fracture in postmenopausal women. Am J Clin Nutr. 1999 Jan;69(1):147-52. PubMed PMID:

186

9925137.

[xvi] Frankenfield D. Energy expenditure and protein requirements after traumatic injury. Nutr Clin Pract. 2006 Oct;21(5):430-7. Review. PubMed PMID: 16998142.

[xvii] Phelan S, Wing RR, Loria CM, Kim Y, Lewis CE. Prevalence and Predictors of Weight-Loss Maintenance in a Bi-Racial Cohort: Results from the CARDIA study. American Journal of Preventive Medicine. 2010;39(6):546-554. doi:10.1016/j.amepre.2010.08.008.

[xviii] https://www.mayoclinic.org/diseases-conditions/torn-meniscus/symptoms-causes/syc-20354818

[xix] Scherbov S and Sanderson WC. Measuring the Speed of Aging across Population Subgroups. PLOS ONE. 2014.

[xx] Goto, Kazushige & Nagasawa, Masanari & Yanagisawa, Osamu & Kizuka, Tomohiro & Ishii, Naokata & Takamatsu, Kaoru. (2004). Muscular Adaptations to Combinations of High- and Low-Intensity Resistance Exercises. Journal of strength and conditioning research / National Strength & Conditioning Association. 18. 730-7. 10.1519/R-13603.1.

[xxi] Omega-3 polyunsaturated fatty acids in physical performance optimization, Mickleborough TD, Journal Title (Medline/Pubmed) accepted abbreviation):Int. J. Sport Nutr. Exerc. Metab.Year: 2013 Volume: 23 Page numbers: 83-96

CPSIA information can be obtained
at www.ICGtesting.com
Printed in the USA
BVHW041920121120
593195BV00027B/463